No Smoke

by

Colin Ward

No Smoke

First published by *In As Many Words* in paperback and digital form.
www.inasmanywords.com

ISBN 978-1-9998089-3-8
Paperback

Cover & book design by Colin Ward

Note:
No performance of any kind, including readings or excerpts, may be given by professional or amateur groups unless a licence has been obtained. This includes not-for-profit, charity and educational groups. Publication of this play does not necessarily indicate its availability for performance. Purchase of a copy of this play, via printed or digital means, does not constitute permission or licence to perform. Please contact the author if you would like to discuss obtaining a licence.

"To protect the innocence of our children
we must protect innocence for us all."

Contents

Characters

David Franklyn. *Ex-youth worker, 30-40*
Ashley Edwards. *A boy, 15*
DS Ellen Cross. *Detective, 30-40*
Michael Edwards. *Ashley's father, 40*
Daniel Fletcher. *Journalist, 25-30*
Ruth Bishop. *Retired detective, 60*

Setting

Public Park; Detective's Office; House; Pub
All the action happens in a small town, large enough to have its own police station with a few detectives, and reasonably close to a major hospital, but not a major city. The setting is a relatively small community where all major locations are accessible on foot.

Original staging

The first production of *No Smoke* was performed at the *Blue Orange Theatre*, Birmingham, from 22nd–24th July 2014, as part of *Birmingham Fest*.

Cast

David Franklyn. *Philip Jennings*

Ashley Edwards. *Harry Yendell*

DS Ellen Cross. *Sarah Gain*

Michael Edwards. *Vincent Clarke*

Daniel Fletcher. *Kieron Attwood*

Ruth Bishop. *Catriona McDonald*

Directed & Designed by

Colin Ward

The development production of the play resulted in the creation of the latest version of the script and helped to shape this first publication.

The play can be performed with the simplest of set, lighting, and optional incidental music. This makes it ideal for small scale and low budget productions, including in schools and educational establishments.

No Smoke

ACT 1

Prologue

Enter Cross and Fletcher.

Fletcher. Recent cases of prolific, predatory paedophiles having abused untold numbers of victims across decades have further raised awareness of the need to strengthen legislation designed to protect our children. Four years ago, Detective Sergeant Ellen Cross was one of the team working on the investigation into David Franklyn. The local youth worker was suspected of sexually assaulting a boy who attended the youth club where he worked. The case rocked the close-knit community and dominated the local news at the time. However, the Crown Prosecution Service were forced to drop the charges on technical grounds and no further action was taken against Mr Franklyn. Detective Cross has been speaking about how better awareness of the behaviour of paedophiles can help alert the public to high-risk individuals gaining access to their children.

Cross. The predatory paedophile will typically follow six key stages in the grooming and abuse of his victims. They are highly manipulative people, good at blending in. The purpose is to make their role and presence in a child's life seem entirely plausible.

Fletcher. How can we identify them?

Cross. Look for key suspicious behaviours. The *first* stage of grooming involves targeting the victim. They'll select a vulnerable, emotionally needy, lonely child – often from broken families. Or parents who both work and have less quality time to give the child. Above all, they choose victims they can get one-to-one contact with in order to create opportunities to abuse the child at a later stage.

Fletcher. Aren't emotionally needy children more likely to be cautious or get scared?

Cross. Most children are trusting, eager to please, and respond well to positive reinforcement. The paedophile will aim to become the helpful, Good Samaritan who is never too busy to lend a hand. They are an over-enthusiastic volunteer, the pleasant neighbour, the new family friend: it's all about making themselves blend in.

David enters as Fletcher and Cross exit.

David. It creeps up, lurking in the shadows, waiting for your back to be turned and your attention elsewhere. You don't even notice it breathing heavily over your shoulder before – before it takes hold. Digs its claws around your shoulders, your neck, your head: it squeezes your chest, and your stomach until you feel sick; it holds your legs so it's heavier to walk; it takes your hands and, puppet-master-like, plays you as a toy. This compulsion, this drive, this energy that both moves you and incapacitates you at the same time. It tells your eyes what to see, your ears what to hear, and your heart what to feel.

David sits down for:

Scene 1

Park

Ashley enters and walks carefully up to the bench where David is sat. He pauses and then finally sits down at the opposite end of the bench. David takes a small notepad out of his pocket and begins writing. He checks his watch and writes down the time, which Ashley notices. David puts the notepad back in his pocket and lets out a quiet but deep, calming sigh.

Ashley. Yeh, I *should* be in school.

David. Oh, that's no business of mine. It's a nice park. Very quiet. A good place to just sit and watch the world go by. Not much to look at, of course. *(Pause)* So, is this what counts as a school field trip these days?

Ashley. I suppose.

David. Well, I guess I'd better give you the guided tour. *(Pointing)* That's Mr Duckling. He's here every day to feed the ducks. That's not unusual on its own, but watch the way he looks around, checks over his shoulder, and tries to subtly drop the bread down the side of his leg so no-one will see him. It's like he's a dirty old man, cheating –

Ashley. – with a duck?

David. I hope not. He's got a flock of geese on the other side of the pond. I figure they don't know about the ducks.

Ashley. Or he's just feeding ducks.

David. Perhaps. Oh, and that's Mr Lens. A private investigator hired by the geese to gather evidence of Mr Duckling's secret double-life.

Ashley. Or he's just bird-watching.

David. Perhaps. And there is Mrs Lead-legs: walks like her legs are filled with lead. It takes her half an hour to walk from one side of the park to the next.

Ashley. She's spying on the bird-watcher guy, right?

David. No, she just walks slowly.

Ashley. Sounds like you've been sitting here a bit too long.

David. You're right: you should be in school.

Ashley. And miss all this fun?

David. I bet it's more interesting than most school trips.

Ashley. That's true.

David. Sometimes you just have to make the most of what's around you. That's what I think, anyway.

Ashley. You know what I think?

David. Shoot.

Ashley. I think you're talking a load of shit.

David. You're probably right.

Ashley. I don't see the point in parks.

David. It's not *what* you see but *how* you see it that matters.

Ashley. What?

David. I'm here pretty much every day. Same park, same bench. Every day I try and look at it in a different way. Occasionally, someone new comes along and the whole place can look completely different. That's when it can get more interesting, trying to work out everyone's little story. Who are they? Why are they here? What do they *usually* do that they have chosen to avoid on this day?

Ashley. You aren't gonna grass me up, are you?

David. To who?

Ashley. School? Cops?

David. As far as I'm concerned, if you want to sit on this public bench any time that's your choice. It doesn't stop me thinking you *should* be at school, though. But, to me, the most interesting people are the ones who look like they *should* be somewhere else.

Ashley. Even you?

David. For me it is more like having no reason to be *anywhere* else.

Ashley. Don't you have a job?

David. Yes, but I just like sitting and watching the world go by. Strangely peaceful, in a way. Gives me time to think.

Ashley. You must have a lot to think about.

David. Don't we all?

Ashley. I guess.

David. Sometimes you can be staring right at the answer and not even realise it.

Ashley. The answer to what?

David. That's the bit that often evades me. I'm not always sure what question I am supposed to be asking.

Ashley. I never knew so much thought went into sitting in a park.

David. Simple places can highlight complicated lives.

Pause. David suddenly starts laughing.

Ashley. What?

David. Our Mr Duckling has finally spotted Mr Lens, and it looks like he doesn't appreciate being caught in shot.

Ashley. This place isn't so boring after all!

David. See, who says you don't learn anything on school trips?

Ashley. *(Getting up)* I should be off, really.

David. Okay.

Ashley. Oh, my mum always says good manners cost nothing, so –

Ashley offers his hand. David pauses for a moment, smiles, and shakes his hand.

David. Quite right. David.

Ashley. Ashley.

David. Nice to meet you.

Ashley. You too.

Ashley exits. David takes out his notepad, checking the time and writes notes as he exits.

Scene 2

Office

Cross. I'll see if I can rustle up a coffee for you, if I can find the bloody kettle.

Bishop. Oh, don't worry about it, '*Starbucks.*'

Cross. Don't call me that! It's wearing a bit thin.

Bishop. Come on, it's funny. You started a craze with
that from your first day.

Cross. I like good coffee! It's not a crime is it?

Bishop. The price is.

Cross. I'm not going to rise to it.

Bishop. So, how is everything going? Nice to see you're
keeping busy.

Cross. Busy is one thing: overworked is another.

Bishop. You love it though. If you're not busy you/
complain…

Cross. …the difference is/ what busy actually means.
Every case I finish creates two caseloads of
paperwork.

Bishop. It's all part of the job, you know that.

Cross. It's getting worse. I can hardly find anything.

Bishop. Are you going to tell me what is *really* on your
mind?

Cross. What do you mean?

Bishop. Don't bother evading the question. Just
remember who taught you –

Cross. –how to invade an evasion – I know.

Bishop. Well?

Cross. It's just an old case I've been mulling over.

Bishop. Which case?

Pause. Cross finds the kettle, but with no base.

Cross. Typical!

Bishop. Oh, that case.

Cross. What is that supposed to mean?

Bishop. You're always the same when that case rears its
ugly head.

Cross. No, I'm not.

Bishop. You evade even the simplest of questions.

Cross. No, I don't.

Bishop. What did you do last night?

Cross finds the base for the kettle.

Cross. Here it is. Milk, sugar?

Bishop. Still taking hours of work home?

Cross. Why does that even matter?

Bishop. Evasion.

Cross. I don't have either.

Bishop. What?

Cross. Milk or sugar.

Bishop. Thank you for making my point.

Cross. I fed the cat, drank some wine, and watched TV.

A pause is filled with a knowing look.

Bishop. And –

Cross. – and did some paperwork.

Bishop. What were you –

Cross. – don't start –

Bishop. – watching on TV?

Cross. The usual rubbish. *(Beat.)* – I don't know! It was just on in the background –

Bishop. Ah, yes.

Cross. Spit it out.

Bishop. It's taking over again.

Cross. *(Playing with engagement ring)* No it isn't.

Bishop. You always play with your ring like that when you lie. And as soon as anyone mentions *Franklyn's* name – see, you can't stand to touch it. *(Pause)* Have you spoken to him recently?

Cross. The case is over.

Bishop. I meant Andy.

Cross. No. He's moved on. You know that.

Bishop. You still wear the ring.

Cross. Well it keeps the perverts away.

Bishop. Surely the irony can't be lost on you.

Cross. Every time: the psychoanalysis.

Bishop. Freudian slip?

Cross. Can we talk about something else?

Bishop. Fine. But until you face it head-on, you're going to be stuck with it. The failure of the Franklyn case and the end of what you and Andy had are linked, in your head, at least.

Cross. Would you like any salt to rub that in with?

Bishop. Ellen, you know that's not what I –

Cross. – Andy left; the case got thrown out at the eleventh hour. Two separate things. Shit happens, and shit doesn't.

Bishop. Just remember – believing in yourself is one thing: believing outside yourself is something completely different.

Cross. I never understood what that meant.

Bishop. We obsess about things outside our control.

Cross reads an email.

Cross. So, the third degree again – is that why you're here?

Bishop. I just came to see how you were. Now I know.

Cross. Well, as you can see, I am – busy. Fine, but busy.

Bishop. That's my cue then. Ellen, remember: keep your friends close –

Cross. – and my enemies –

Bishop. – neatly filed away under 'case closed'. I'll see you soon.

Cross. Don't be a stranger.

Bishop exits. Cross thinks carefully for a moment, collects her things and exits.

Scene 3

Edwards Home

Michael enters, goes straight to a side table with various bottles and pours himself double-vodka. Ashley enters.

Ashley. How's mum?

Michael. No change.

Ashley. She's gonna be alright though? Dad?

Michael. It's early days.

Ashley. Can I come and see her with you tomorrow?

Michael. She's really not well. I explained, didn't I? She's still in a coma, Ash, she –

Ashley. – I don't care about that, she's my mum.

Michael. It's just hard to see her so still, so quiet; hooked up to all those wires, tubes –

Ashley. You always say I have to be strong.

Michael. I know I do. And I *will* take you.

Ashley. When?

Michael. When she's ready! – Sorry, I'm just so tired and – and there's nothing I can do. I just feel so helpless. It's driving me crazy.

Ashley. Why her, Dad? Why did it have to happen to her?

Michael. I've been asking myself that same question over and over. But it was just a terrible accident.

Ashley. It's not fair.

Michael. No, it isn't. *(Pause)* Have you heard from your brother at all?

Ashley. No.

Michael. I tried calling him, but you know what he's like.

Ashley. Does he even know about mum?

Michael. I left him a message. And you sent him a text, and an email, right?

Ashley. Yeh, but he's too busy with all his uni mates to care enough to call me back.

Michael. You have to give him time. Steve needs his own space.

Ashley. Why?

Michael. We've been through this. One day you'll go flying the nest too, going off to uni, getting a job, whatever it is you want to do.

Ashley. I'd come back if I had to, though.

Michael. And so will Steve. But for now, we are doing just fine, aren't we? We're a team, remember.

Ashley. No, the team was always you and Steve, with me tagging along. Now he's gone, there is no *team*.

Michael. Ash, you held the team together. You, me, Steve.

Ashley. And mum?

Michael. Of course.

Ashley. But she's not here either.

Michael. All the more reason we've got to stick together right now.

Ashley. So, let's stick together and *both* go to see mum. Like you said – we're a team.

Michael. Ash, it's not that simple.

Ashley. I bet you'd take Steve if he bothered to come back, wouldn't you?

Michael. Ashley, please! You know how much Steve wanted to get away from *here*: always had done since – it was hard for Steve – for all of us – all those prying eyes. Even worse with – well, *(with venom)* HIM still living around here. If I could turn the clock back, maybe there are some things I'd do. I don't know. But when is life ever simple? – Anyway, how is school?

Ashley. Fine.

Michael. I was thinking of phoning the school to let them know about mum, just in case –

Ashley. I'm not a kid, dad. I don't need people looking after me.

Michael. You may not think so, but if they knew, maybe they could cut you a little slack or –

Ashley. I don't need it.

Michael. What if I just had a quiet word with your form tutor?

Ashley. No, dad! Just leave it, alright?

Michael. Okay, I will. I just remember how hard it was when you were younger and what happened with Steve came out. Everyone wanted to know everything, and no-one had a sense of privacy. I don't want that happening again, okay? So, if anyone gives you any/ hassle…

Ashley. ...I'll/ come straight to you, dad, you know I will.

Michael. You've got to be careful who you talk to.

Ashley. What do you mean by that?

Michael. People aren't always what they seem at first. I don't want you growing up paranoid, but I also don't want you growing up unprepared.

Ashley. For what?

Michael. For the world. The risks. What's out there – *who* is out...I don't know. I'm rambling, I'm tired. Listen, let me check with the hospital, see how mum is getting on, and then we'll both go and see her, together. Okay?

Ashley. Okay. *(Moves to exit but turns back.)* Everything's gonna be okay, isn't it?

Michael. Yeh.

Ashley exits.

Michael. I hope so.

Exit

Scene 4

Pub

David is sitting alone, with his notepad on the table. Cross enters with a drink in her hand.

David. Detective Cross.

Cross. Mr Franklyn.

David. Off duty?

Cross. Excuse me?

David. Wouldn't want to be caught drinking on duty, would you? You never know what people might think – or say – about that.

Cross. May I join you?

David. A dalliance with the devil? Has Hell frozen over already?

Cross. Not that I know of.

David. Good. I wouldn't want you catching a cold now, would I? So, what brings you here?

Cross. Passing and fancied a drink. That's what a pub is for, isn't it?

David. You never were a good liar.

Cross. Not as good as you?

David. Impressive deflection. Within a few moments we'll be up to our necks in an interrogation. So, have you tracked me down in your official capacity, or is it merely on a social basis?

Cross. Why do you stick around? Didn't you ever think of moving away?

David. This is where I live.

Cross. Surely it would have been easier to move on.

David. Easier for whom, I ask?

Cross. Everyone.

David. Including me?

Cross. It can't be easy spending your time trying to hide where you are so well known?

David. Who said I was trying to hide?

Cross. You're not that easy to track down.

David. I'm flattered by your virtuous diligence. Off duty, of course. Are you going to forego the platitudes and get on with it?

Cross. I have been tipped off by a source that you might be engaging in, shall we say, behaviours that could be a little too open to negative perceptions.

David. A little off duty gossip and you commence a personal manhunt?

Cross. It's hardly a manhunt. But do you think it wise to be seen so openly engaging in social meetings with boys? Especially given your reputation.

David. Social meetings?

Cross. You were in the park this morning, weren't you?

David. Are you asking me that as an officer or as an off-duty officer?

Cross. Just answer the question.

David. I'm in the park every day.

Cross. But today you were seen talking to a boy.

David. I speak to many people.

Cross. We both know that's not true.

David. I talk to members of the public, in a public park, so publicly that if anyone was to see me and make a note of it, they could do so.

Cross. You are being obtrusive.

David. You are being intrusive.

Cross. You were seen talking to a boy – a little unwise, don't you think?

David. To have talked, or to have been seen?

Cross. He was your type, though, wasn't he?

David. And by that you mean –

Cross. – the right age. Men like you fixate on a type,
don't they?

David. One could almost be forgiven –

Cross. – I doubt it –

David. – for thinking it sounds more like you are the
one who is fixating.

Cross. Really?

David. You hear that a man has been seen talking to a
boy and the first thing that pops into *your* mind is sex.
Perhaps we should reflect more on what that says
about you.

Cross. You being seen talking alone with a boy could
easily be perceived as –

David. Grooming?

Cross. Your word.

David. You either think I've been grooming or you
don't. Perhaps you should have come to arrest me
whilst being on-duty. That way this conversation
might not be perceived as an obsessed, off-duty
copper trying to illicit a false confession of a crime
during a personal manhunt based on spurious
rumour.

Cross. Don't try and get clever with me.

David. Did you wait until you spotted your target before
you bought your white wine spritzer?

Cross. Look, you should take my advice –

David. The only thing to do with good advice is to pass
it on. Oscar Wilde.

Cross. Don't have private conversations –

David. – in public –

Cross. – with boys.

David. Would it be ok if I had conversations with girls?
Or, what about holding conversations with boys
somewhere a little more private?

Cross. Just remember, I am watching you.

David. Yes, Sergeant. With everyone else's eyes but your
own.

Cross. Tread carefully, Franklyn.

David. What pisses you off the most: the fact that you
couldn't pin it on me four years ago, or the feeling
that you are way out of your depth now?

*David finishes his drink, puts his glass down, and begins writing
in his notebook as he exits.*
Enter Fletcher.

Fletcher. Detective.

Cross. Mr Fletcher.

Fletcher. How have you been keeping?

Cross. Just fine. What are you after now?

Fletcher. Nothing, nothing!

Cross. You're always leeching after your next scoop.

Fletcher. Can't two public servants have a civil
conversation?

Cross. Firstly, you are not a public servant –

Fletcher. – my readers would beg to differ –

Cross. – and secondly, any conversation with you is
usually a few keystrokes away from a formal
reprimand!

Fletcher. Oh, so harsh, so unfair, so –

Cross. – what do you want?

Fletcher. Did you have a nice little chat with Mr
Franklyn?

Cross. I have no idea what you're talking about.

Fletcher. That's not fair! You've gotta play a bit of give-and-take.

Cross. I have no intention of falling into the trap of taking from you again.

Fletcher. You've already taken.

Cross. I don't have time for this.

Fletcher. But you do have time to follow up a nice anonymous tip-off about a known local paedophile hanging around public parks to chat to boys?

Cross. That was your handy-work then?

Fletcher. I was doing my bit for the community. Come on, just a few questions.

Cross. Ask whatever questions you want.

Fletcher. See, I knew you'd be a good sport.

Cross. I never said I would answer them.

Fletcher. Are you currently investigating Mr Franklyn?

Cross. If Mr Franklyn was under investigation by the local police – which I have *not* said that he is – I wouldn't discuss that with you.

Fletcher. What was the purpose of your conversation with Mr Franklyn?

Cross. I was merely in the same pub, off-duty, having a drink. No conversation, no purpose.

Fletcher. You are hard work today, aren't you? Come on, give me something, anything.

Cross. There is nothing to give.

Fletcher. *"Local Police Officer Tracks Down Old Nemesis."*

Cross. I'm not listening.

Fletcher. *"Above and Beyond: Off Duty Police Protecting the Public."*

Cross. You are incorrigible!

Fletcher. *"Police Pursue Paedos for Pleasure"*?

Cross. *(Indignant.)* Goodbye Mr Fletcher.

Fletcher. Too far? Or, was it too close?

Cross. Try as hard as you like, you're not getting any form of statement from me.

Fletcher. Just a comment about your current investigation into Mr Franklyn?

Cross. It is *not* an investigation – it was just an informal conversation.

Fletcher. So, it *was* a conversation then? Now we're getting somewhere.

Cross. I had a brief off-duty conversation with a man in a pub.

Fletcher. About?

Cross. Nothing that concerns you.

Fletcher. Concerned that my favourite law enforcement officer is socialising with known paedophiles?

Cross. Print that and you'll find yourself reporting on your own libel case.

Fletcher. Fine, have it your way. God, what has changed? You used to be so much more helpful, so much more – dare I say it – fun! Did failure turn you gritty and bitter?

Cross. Mr Fletcher –

Fletcher. – Daniel –

Cross. Mr Fletcher – I admire your enthusiasm, I really do. And I guess I owe you a thank you for the information you gave me –

Fletcher. – excellent! Let's go out for dinner.

Cross. Are you asking me out on a date?

Fletcher. A drink, then?

Cross. With you?

Fletcher. Ok, a cone of chips?

Cross. You're barking up the wrong tree.

Fletcher. Just a walk to Tesco and back?

Cross. Daniel –

Fletcher. – live a little! Come and get a sausage roll at the self-service checkout.

Cross. You're sounding desperate now.

Fletcher. Am I? I can beg. I will, if you want me to.

Cross. Stop it, will you?! Dan, I like you, but you are more like an irritating little brother.

Fletcher. Ouch! You make it sound incestuous!

Cross. You're more trouble than you're worth.

Fletcher. *(With more seriousness)* You know, if you really want rid of him –

Cross. – I know what you are going to say –

Fletcher. – no, you/ don't…

Cross. …vigilante/ action is illegal and –

Fletcher. – not what I was going to suggest. Look, we can't make anything up, and we can't dig up old cases and try and re-hash coverage on them. He's too smart for that, and he really would have my balls for libel action. But there's nothing stopping me writing an article on protecting children from paedophiles is there? It's all in the public/ interest…

Cross. …you/ are playing with fire, you know that?

Fletcher. And you are just trying to blow out my flame.

Cross gets up to leave.

Cross. No, I'm trying to stop you getting burnt. And me.

Fletcher. I'll keep my eyes and ears open. If anything
crops up, I'll let you know.

Cross. That won't be necessary.

Fletcher. In that case, in the absence of necessity I offer
only my pleasure.

The scene changes and David enters.

David. It's a very different kind of conversation, talking
to a child. Listening to them. Finding a way to meet
them half way by using their language but also lifting
them up and giving them something new to
understand. It's getting to know them, learning about
them as an individual. The more you know the further
you can get, but carefully, always feeling natural,
healthy, safe. Relationships must feel mutual. A step
in the wrong direction, a little too much pressure, or a
line crossed too soon could be perceived as alarming.
You don't want that. And they don't need that. You
must appear focused on entirely on their needs: that's
the only way it can work.

*Cross and Fletcher move to previous positions either side of the
stage.*

Cross. In the second stage of grooming, the paedophile
gathers information, allowing them to get closer to
the child. Their family, their hobbies and interests:
anything they can use to progress the relationship. If
they know what the child likes, they will be better
placed to buy their affection later. If they know the
child's fears, they will be more able to appear to be a
protector.

Fletcher. Don't parents or other adults notice them getting too close?

Cross. They must act with care not to appear too *over-familiar*. They cannot be too affectionate, certainly not in front of anyone – too much touching, petting, physical play and this could arouse suspicion. They must put themselves in a position in the child's life that makes them welcome and wanted.

Fletcher. Surely you'd notice someone hanging around too much? Any parent who truly loves their child/…

Cross. …/loves to see their child smile and be happy. If the paedophile can make this happen, casually, apparently in an appropriate way, why would anyone suspect them? That's how they do it. They build up the adult's *and* the child's trust and then they abuse it.

Exit.

Scene 5

Park

Ashley is sitting on the bench, alone, staring out into the distance.

David. It's not going to get any closer, you know?

Ashley. What?

David. The world out there, in the distance. No matter how hard you stare, it never gets any closer. But I think if you stare hard enough out into the distance your stare can shoot all the way round the Earth until it comes right up behind you and smacks you in the head.

Ashley. That's not very likely, is it?

David. Something not being likely doesn't mean it's impossible.

Ashley. Well, it is because even if we could shoot something out of our eyes it would smash into a mountain or something before it gets all the way round the planet.

David. Fair enough. *(Pause)* Two days on the trot – you must have a lot on your mind.

Ashley. Not really.

David. Okay.

Ashley. Why do people always want to talk?

David. I guess they believe talking helps.

Ashley. It doesn't, though.

David. That depends on what you want to get out of it.

Ashley. Doesn't make problems go away.

David. No, not always. Sometimes talking can make it seem like there are even more problems. But talking things through with someone could help you get it straight in your head.

Ashley. You saying I've got problems?

David. Sorry, I didn't mean *you* – I meant in general. Saying something out loud and getting someone to listen can help give you a new perspective.

Ashley. Well, that's the problem, getting people to listen. No-one listens. *(Pause)* – What? – What did I say? – I didn't mean *you* had to stop talking. – Well, say something!

David. So, now you don't like it when I stop talking?

Ashley. You were freaking me out! I thought I'd offended you or /something…

David. ...I was/listening.

Ashley. To what?

David. *(Amused)* To you! You said no-one ever listens to you – I was listening.

Ashley. Oh. *(Pause)* Adults! I thought you were giving me the silent treatment.

David. I was. Look. *(Getting out his notepad and showing)* Did you know that the words 'silent' and 'listen' contain the same letters?

Ashley. That's cool. But I think I prefer it when you talk.

David. I choose to take that as a compliment! Teenagers! Talking, no talking – jeeze!

Ashley. You don't seem to spend much time at work – is it a shit job?

David. You don't seem to spend much time at school – is it a shit school?

Ashley. I've only missed a couple of days – I don't think anyone will be bothered.

David. The longer you stay away, the harder it is to go back.

Ashley. To school?

David. Well, to anything, really.

Ashley. Well, I don't care.

David. Yes you do.

Ashley. No, I don't care about my shitty school.

David. You care about something or you wouldn't be here. *(Pause.)* So, what is it you care about that makes you/ come here...

Ashley. ...what do/ you do for work then?

David. I'm a writer.

Ashley. Do you write books like Harry Potter and Game of Thrones?

David. No, nothing that glamorous. I just write short articles.

Ashley. Oh, like a news reporter?

David. Good God, no. I'm sent products to write an article about, giving my opinion on how good they are. The people I work for like me to write nice things so other people will buy their products.

Ashley. Like advertising, then?

David. Well not/ exactly…

Ashley. …I'd/ love a job in advertising.

David. Really?

Ashley. I like the idea of being able to persuade people. I could test games and then tell people about the best ones to buy. If anyone wanted to know which is the best game to buy, they'd come to me for advice.

David. Like 'Which?'.

Ashley. Games magazines and stuff.

David. Yes, I mean like the magazine: 'Which?'.

Ashley. I dunno – a games/ one…

David. *(Laughing)* Sounds good.

Ashley. And I could tell games designers how to make their games better.

David. Why not be a games designer yourself?

Ashley. You think I could do that?

David. Why not?

Ashley. What do you have to be good at for that?

David. Well, I assume you'd have to be good with computers, art, and probably maths.

Ashley. Well, I know computers, and I can draw pretty
well. Maths? That's what they invented calculators for.
You might have seen them – it's a modern invention.

David. Oh, the age jokes. How original.

Ashley. Grandpa!

David. Enough of that! I'm barely old enough to be
your dad. *(An awkward silence.)* I get the feeling I've
just put my foot in it.

Ashley. I don't like people talking about my family.

David. That's okay. Sorry if I've spoken out of turn.

Ashley. It's ok.

David. *(Carefully)* You talk *to* your family, though? Right?

Ashley. Not really.

David. Oh?

Ashley. Brother's gone to uni; dad's mostly out.

David. And what about that wonderful mum who we
have to thank for your good manners?

Ashley. She's – well, she – Just leave it, alright?

David. Okay.

Ashley. Do you talk to complete strangers about your
family?

David. That's a fair point. I apologise if you felt I was
intruding.

Pause.

Ashley. Mum's in hospital.

David. Oh. I'm sorry.

Ashley. No, you're not. You don't know my mum – or
me, really.

David. You're right. I didn't mean for that to *sound* false.
But my sympathy – that is genuine.

Ashley. I don't want your sympathy.

David. Well, you're going to get it whether you want it or not. *(Beat.)* Do you mind if I ask what happened?

Ashley. Car accident.

David. How is she doing?

Ashley. Dad says she's in a coma.

David. Well, I wish there was something I could say/ but…

Ashley. …there's/ nothing to say.

David. All I know about comas is that doctors think the patient – your mum – can hear your voice, maybe sense your presence.

Ashley. Can she?

David. Apparently so. How long has /she…?

Ashley. …the/ weekend. It happened on Saturday night.

David. Oh, I see. I guess having the time to visit your mum is more important than school at the moment.

Ashley. If my dad would let me.

Cross enters and watches, keeping out of their site.

David. What do you mean?

Ashley. He says it will be too upsetting for me. Treats me like a stupid little kid. I hate it.

David. Well, I'm sure he's just trying to do what he thinks is right for his family.

Ashley. I don't want to talk about it, anyway.

David. Ok, that's no problem.

David opens his notepad, writes something, tears out the page, and gives it piece of paper to Ashley.

Ashley. What's this?

David. You can call any time.

Ashley. Why have you given me this?

David. Because whether you believe it or not, it *is* good to talk.

Ashley. Okay. Thanks. *(Beat.)* Do you carry that notepad everywhere? It makes you look like a reporter!

David. I choose *not* to take that as a compliment. Look, I've got to be off, I'm afraid.

Ashley. Okay. See you tomorrow?

David. No, you won't, young man: you'll be in school.

Ashley. See you around then.

David. *(Puts a hand lightly on Ashley's shoulder.)* I hope your mum gets better soon. See you around. *(Begins to exit; pause.)* Ashley. It was good to talk: even better to listen.

David exits. Ashley puts the piece of paper in his pocket as Cross approaches.

Cross. Do you mind if I sit here?

Ashley. Free world.

Cross. Yes, it is. *(Pause)* Are you here on your own then?

Ashley looks around and then at Cross, who acknowledges the ridiculous question.

Ashley. Can I help you?

Cross. I don't know.

Ashley. You a hooker or something?

Cross. What?! No! – Do I look like a hooker to you?

Ashley. I dunno. What's a hooker look like?

Cross. I'm not going to answer that.

Ashley. I suppose a bit more slutty than you.

Cross. Only a *bit* more slutty? Thanks. – Shouldn't you
be in school?

Ashley. Don't you start. Are you're a cop, or something?

Cross. Actually –

Ashley. – you don't look like one.

Cross. Nice to know I look more like a hooker than a
copper. I'm a detective. We get to wear mufti.

Ashley. What?

Cross. Never mind. Anyway.

Cross shows Ashley her ID.

Ashley. Does that mean I'm in more shit for skipping
school?

Cross. Make a habit of it, do you?

Ashley. No.

Cross. Then consider this your lucky day. I'm not in the
arresting mood. But don't do it again – or I'll have to
pop a cap in y'ass. – Sorry. Not cool. *(Recoiling.)* But
I'll turn a blind eye just this once. *(Pause)* Why are you
here, though?

Ashley. Just watching the world go by.

Cross. Seen anything, or anyone in particular?

Ashley. It's a bit weird for a detective to hang around,
isn't it? You under-cover?

Cross. Maybe I am.

Ashley. Well, you're not very good at it since you've
already told me who you are.

Cross. A good point. Maybe I should arrest you to keep
you quiet, or I could drag you home to your parents!

Ashley. No, don't! My dad doesn't need the hassle. He'll
go mental.

Cross. I was joking, calm down. Your dad – easily
wound up, is he?

Ashley. I guess. Yeh. It's just me and him at the
moment.

Cross. What about your mum?

Ashley. She's – *(reluctantly)* not well.

Cross. Not serious, I hope.

Ashley. She's in hospital. In a coma.

Cross. Oh, God! What happened?

Ashley. Car accident. I don't know much about it, really.
Dad just doesn't need the extra stress of some copper
grassing me up.

Cross. Understandable. How are you holding up?

Ashley. I'm fine.

Cross. And what about your brother?

Ashley. What?

Cross. You don't remember me, do you? I was the
detective who investigated what happened to your
brother.

Ashley. Oh right. You're *that* copper.

Cross. How is Steven?

Ashley. I should go.

Cross. What happened to watching the world go by?

Ashley. It's always better when I don't have to talk to
anyone.

Cross. Always?

Ashley. Look, just don't tell my dad I was skiving, okay?
Please.

Cross. I'm not here to harass you or start telling tales to
your dad. I just saw you and thought I'd check if you
were okay, that's all.

Ashley. Why wouldn't I be?

Cross. For one thing, you should be in school. I might not be reporting it this time, but I couldn't exactly walk away, could I?

Ashley. I suppose.

Cross. You didn't say how your brother is. And I'm only asking as *me*, not as me-the-copper.

Ashley. He's gone to uni.

Cross. That's good.

Ashley. I guess. For him.

Cross. It can't have been easy for –

Ashley. I've got to go.

Cross. Okay. But wait a second. Look, take my card. I know you don't want to talk, but just in case – well, take it anyway.

Ashley. Okay. Whatever.

Cross. I hope your mum gets well soon. Look after yourself, ok?

Ashley. Yeh. Thanks.

Ashley exits. Cross remains seated, thinks for a moment, and then exits.

Scene 6

Pub

Fletcher. Quite the regular haunt for you, isn't it, Mr Franklyn?

David. Do we know each other?

Fletcher. Everyone knows who you are, don't they?

David. Ah, yes – now I recall.

Fletcher. Good!

David. When someone drags your name through the dirt they do tend to stick in your mind.

Fletcher. Didn't you ever think of just moving on, getting away from it all, starting afresh somewhere else? It must be uncomfortable, everyone knowing what happened.

Pause.

David. What do you want, Fletcher?

Fletcher. Honestly?

David. Yes. Go on; enlighten me.

Fletcher. Everyone would be happier if you found a big, dirty rock to crawl under somewhere far away from here. Especially far away from any kids.

David. That's the truth, is it?

Fletcher. Oh, come on! You live alone – no family or friends. Not working in Youth Clubs any more, are you? Or doing the private tutoring? Not anywhere savvy enough to take a look at your DBS. They know *what* they have in their midst. The word: *paedophile*. It has a ring to it, don't you think?

David. So, why do you lower your voice every time you say it? Is that a kind of reporter's irony? Type big: speak small.

Fletcher. There's no need to create a scene.

David. Because you already told the story?

Fletcher. The fact of/ the matter…

David. …an/ interesting word: / fact…

Fletcher. …the/ fact of the matter is that I know you've
started your games again. Talking to boys sat alone in
the park. You don't even seem to want to hide your
sickness.

David. Sickness?

Fletcher. Sickness, compulsion, or whatever excuse you
try to use for really want from kids.

David. You just love to spin the stories so fast your
readers are too dizzy to see straight, let alone notice
the absurdity of what is staring right back at them.

Fletcher. How can you sit here and spout such bullshit?

David. Yet more reporter's irony?

Fletcher. Look, I'm not going to entertain your ego any
more. Ellen doesn't need you getting up to your old
tricks on her patch.

David. Ellen? First name basis. The press and the police
do work so *closely* together.

Fletcher. You're on dodgy grounds passing comment
on appropriate relationships.

David. Haven't you got anything better to do with your
time than harass me?

Fletcher. You stop your hunt and I'll stop mine. I have
no problem making your life a lot more
uncomfortable than it already is.

David. Is that a threat? Let's get something very clear,
Mr Fletcher: I don't welcome your company, I don't
appreciate your tone, and I don't wish for you to
speak to me or approach me again. Harassment never
looks good on anyone's card. Are you going to write
that down?

Fletcher. I'm not harassing you.

David. And you're not going to. Are you?

Fletcher. Is that a threat?

David. *(Getting up to leave)* Good evening, Mr Fletcher.

Fletcher. You don't intimidate me, Franklyn.

David. Yes, I do.

David exits.

Scene 7

Edwards House

Michael enters with a cup of coffee.

Michael. It's not one of your fancy coffee shop bought ones, but –

Cross. I can't believe you remember that.

Michael. Well, you always seemed to have one of them with you. Isn't it funny the little details you remember when you face – well, you know?

Cross' mobile phone rings.

Cross. It was a traumatic time for everyone. *(She cancels the call.)* – Sorry about that.

Michael. It's no problem – I know you're busy. Speaking of which I'm not in for long myself. I have to go out and see my wife soon.

Cross. Oh yes, of course.

Michael. You know about my wife?

Cross. I meant that I wouldn't want to hold you up.

Michael. She's in hospital. In a bad way. A coma.

Cross. I'm so sorry to hear that.

Ashley enters off stage and calls in.

Ashley. *(Offstage)* Dad?
Michael. My youngest.

Ashley enters.

Ashley. I thought you'd be with – *(Sees Cross)* Oh.
Michael. Not sure if you'd remember Detective Cross, Ash.
Cross. Well, I certainly remember you – how you've grown. *(Winks.)* Such a *long time* since I saw you last.
Ashley. Yeh?
Cross. It must be about four years.
Ashley. Oh, right.
Michael. About that.
Cross. Your dad was just telling me about your mum. It must be really hard on the three of you.
Ashley. Three?
Cross. Your brother?
Michael. Steve's at University now. I think it was good for him to get away, start being more independent. It's not been easy on him, or any of us. I don't mean to sound rude, detective, but why are you here? Is something wrong?
Cross. No, nothing's wrong. Actually, I need your help.
Michael. You're re-opening the case? You've caught him at it again, haven't you?
Cross. Well, not exactly.
Michael. It is about him though, isn't it?
Cross. I am just trying to piece together some facts –
Michael. – I knew this would happen if he walked free.
Ashley. Dad, don't –

Michael. – everything he's put us through: that's what
led to my wife's accident, you know?
Ashley. Dad!
Cross. How so?
Michael. He drove her to it.
Cross. The accident?
Ashley. Dad, shouldn't you be getting to –
Michael. – what he did to this family, and then sticking
around after he got away with it – that's what drove
her to it: the depression, the anti-depressants –
Cross. – and you think that caused your wife's accident?
Michael. She should never have been driving. The drugs
made her drowsy, messed up her system. I told her
she shouldn't be driving.
Cross. Oh, right.
Michael. I bet your lot will want to question her as soon
as she's opened her eyes –
Cross. Was anyone else was hurt?
Michael. No.
Cross. In that case, try not to worry about it.
Michael. That's easy for you to say.
Cross. You're right. I apologise. Anyway, there's just this
other issue.
Michael. Right?
Cross. Have you seen Mr Franklyn since the case?
Michael. A few times.
Cross. Did he approach you? Talk to you?
Michael. I don't think he'd dare. In all truth it's taken a
lot of strength not to do something I might regret.
Cross. I can imagine it has. *(To Ashley)* I doubt you'd
recognise him really. You never met him, did you? –

In truth, I've never really understood why he stayed in the area.

Michael. Rubbing our noses in it? Doesn't bother him. Some kind of power trip.

Cross. To be honest, I'm sticking my neck on the line here, Mr Edwards. I shouldn't really be having this conversation with you at all.

Michael. 'Off-the-record' chat, then?

Cross. He's been brought to my attention again.

Michael. On the prowl, is he? You haven't caught him with another victim? –

Cross. – it would wise to be vigilant, just until I –

Michael. – because if he so much as comes near my Ashley, I swear –

Cross. – don't worry: I assure you I'll keep Ashley safe.

Michael. Would that be the same assurance you gave me that Franklyn would be locked up?

Ashley. Dad, stop it.

Cross. No, Ashley, it's a fair point. If you see anything, hear anything, or if he approaches either of you at all, then you must contact me.

Michael. Why would he approach us after such a long time? Has he been around *here*?

Cross. He's not been seen down your street. I made it clear to him that it would be a very bad idea to come anywhere near you or your family.

Michael. Good. That pervert ruined my son, my family, and he's been walking the streets a free man ever since. You talk of assurances. What about Justice?

Cross. I can appreciate your anger – and I'd feel the same way. Now we know more about him –

Michael. – you won't make the same mistakes?

Cross. We can stop him before he even gets to harm anyone else.

Michael. Well, you go, you find him, and you tell him that if he comes near my family again –

Cross. – I'm keeping a close eye on him.

Michael. Good.

Cross. Here's my card. You can call me directly if you have any concerns.

Michael. Okay, thank you. Sorry, but I've really got to go and see my wife –

Cross. – I understand completely. I apologise if my coming round has stirred up even more stress, what with your –

Michael. – no, it's fine. I'm just a bit on edge and –

Cross. – of course. I won't hold you up. – Good to see you again, Ashley: all grown up.

Michael shows Cross out. As they exit:

Michael. Thanks, anyway. You know?

Cross. No trouble at all. Thanks for your time. And I hope your wife gets better soon.

Ashley takes the piece of paper David gave him out of his pocket, but quickly puts it back as Michael enters again.

Michael. Right, I need to go out, and when I get back I think we need to have a little chat.

Ashley. Why?

Michael. Because I need to know that you understand the risks out there.

Ashley. I can look after myself, dad, I'm not stupid.

Michael. All the same. We need to stay protected.

Ashley. From who?

Michael. The world's a complicated place, Ashley. Sometimes you have to learn how to keep your friends close, but your enemies closer.

Ashley. Why keep your enemies closer, though?

Michael. To keep an eye on them and what they're up to.

Ashley. Is that why *he* sticks around then?

Michael. We aren't his enemies.

Ashley. We reported him to the police.

Michael. And rightly so. What he put us through, Ash. All of us. But if we stick together, as a team, he can't hurt us any more, can he?

Ashley. No.

Michael. Look, I need to go. You'll be okay, right?

Ashley. Can I come with you?

Michael. I just need a little time to myself.

Ashley. You're not going to see mum?

Michael. I need to clear my head first. Okay?

Ashley. Yeh.

Michael. You're a good lad, Ashley, always sticking by your old dad. Sometimes I think I don't deserve you.

Michael Exits. Ashley looks at the phone number again and thinks about dialling. He stops and puts it away; exit.

Scene 8

Pub

Fletcher is already sitting down as Bishop enters, talking on the phone.

Bishop. Ellen, it's Ruth – *again*. Stop cancelling my calls. Call me back.

She hangs up.

Fletcher. Detective – sorry, *former*, Detective Bishop! What brings you to this neck of the woods? Can I buy you a drink?

Bishop. No, I'm not staying. Thank you. Have you seen Detective Cross?

Fletcher. Why do you ask?

Bishop. Why don't you answer?

Fletcher. You know, I do find it interesting it that Ellen's esteemed mentor reappears on the scene just at the same time that our dear Detective has rekindled her interest in Mr Franklyn.

Bishop. Your point?

Fletcher. It's not a point, it's an observation.

Bishop. Well, since you clearly haven't seen her, I'll be heading off.

Fletcher. Such a shame. I was going to ask you for a statement about work on the paedo-prowl.

Bishop. There is no need to be vulgar. And you should just leave Detective Cross to get on with her work.

Fletcher. So, she *is* investigating Mr Franklyn again?

Bishop. You know full well that I never said that.

Fletcher. But she's definitely taking an interest again, isn't she?

Bishop. No comment.

Fletcher. I have heard of women playing hard to get, but you – you're just playing hard to get past. How I do like a challenge.

Bishop. Mr Fletcher, I think you over-estimate the lure of your infatuation with Ellen.

Fletcher. Infatuation? I call it inspiration.

Bishop. Oh, please.

Fletcher. She is a wonderful woman.

Bishop. And she doesn't need you sniffing around.

Fletcher. Now who's being vulgar? Besides, I don't sniff, I merely publish facts supplied to me by a reliable source.

Bishop. Source? A moment ago you were calling her your inspiration.

Fletcher. She's a *source* of inspiration. Thanks to Ellen's generosity, I have often achieved more in the public interest than the public realises it is interested in. Franklyn is a case in point. His face was as guilty as sin.

Bishop. Not in the eyes of the law.

Fletcher. And who needs the eyes of the law when you have the glare of public on your side? Now, with this new information –

Bishop. What new information?

Fletcher. Hasn't your protégé told you? Franklyn's on the hunt again. Seen talking to a boy, alone, in the park just yesterday.

Bishop. Hardly enough to act upon.

Fletcher. Enough for Ellen to feel compelled to have a *conversation* with him though.

Bishop. When?

Fletcher. Yesterday. Now, imagine what the world could be like if everyone stopped thinking child abuse is always someone else's problem.

Bishop. Don't try to patronise me, Fletcher.

Fletcher. The legal system fails to control these dangerous individuals in our midst, so what else are we to do? Just sit back and accept it? But if Ellen went to meet Franklyn, she clearly has an agenda of her own.

Bishop. I am sure she has her reasons.

Fletcher. And I am sure that is why she went to see Mr Edwards, too.

Bishop. What? When?

Fletcher. Oh, so *now* I'm supposed to be *your* source?

Bishop. If you knew, why didn't you try and stop her?

Fletcher. You know what Ellen is like when she gets ideas in her head.

Bishop. Yes, and that's why *I* don't bloody place them there.

Michael Enters the bar, sitting down with a drink.

Fletcher. Speak of the devil.

Bishop. Mr Fletcher, if you care at all about Ellen you'll know when to back off.

Fletcher. Send Ellen my love.

Bishop exits.

Fletcher. Penny for your thoughts.

Michael. Excuse me?

Fletcher. You look like a man with a lot on his mind.

Michael. Do we know each other? You look familiar.

Fletcher. I guess I must have one of those faces.

Michael. No, we've met – I just can't quite place you.

Fletcher. Okay, I confess. You've got me. I'm a
    journalist.

Michael. Yes, now I remember you.

Fletcher. How are things?

Michael. I'm not making a statement.

Fletcher. Good, because I am not taking one.

Michael. I'm just here for a quiet drink, that's all.

Fletcher. Me too. – Avoiding your better half?

Michael. Hardly. You?

Fletcher. Well, I do have my eye on a local feisty bird.
    She split up with her boyfriend a few years ago so I
    figure I've got to be safe from the rebound factor by
    now.

Michael. Don't be so sure. They always come with some
    baggage.

Fletcher. I like a challenge.

Michael. You want a challenge? Settle down, get
    married, have kids. Life is a challenge.

Fletcher. I'll drink to that. Still, you'd better not stay out
    too late, though, right?

Michael. She won't mind.

Fletcher. Oh, now sir, don't mistake my ringless finger
    for ignorance. They *always* mind.

Michael. Not when they are lying in hospital.

Fletcher. Shit – you're joking?

Michael. Nope.

Fletcher. Sorry. That's a bit rough. What happened? If you don't mind my asking.

Michael. If I see you get your notepad out I'll shove it so far up your arse –

Fletcher. – I'll be shitting reports out for a month.

Michael. Something like that.

Fletcher. Funnily enough, my editor says that's all I do. I'm just asking man-to-man, but if you're not –

Michael. She ran her car off the road.

Fletcher. Jesus. Your kids – they weren't? –

Michael. – no, she was on her own, no other cars involved.

Fletcher. I bet they must be finding all this a bit rough too.

Michael. They're holding up. My youngest wants to visit his mum but I just can't bring myself to let him see her like that.

Fletcher. Where's she being treated?

Michael. That's a journalist's question.

Fletcher. Sorry, force of habit. What about the eldest?

Michael. He's at university.

Fletcher. Doing well for himself, then?

Michael. Yeh.

Fletcher. And how old is your youngest now?

Michael. Ashley? Fifteen.

Fletcher. I don't have my own kids, but I bet they grow up fast.

Michael. Too fast.

Fletcher. Never stops you protecting them, though, does it?

Michael. No, it doesn't.

Fletcher. What happened to that Franklyn in the end?

Michael. I would have thought a man like you would have kept track.

Fletcher. No disrespect, but when a story loses steam, you tend to –

Michael. – stop paying attention?

Fletcher. Well, more like running out of things you can write about – things you are allowed to write about.

Michael. He stuck around.

Fletcher. Really?

Michael. Why not? He got away with it. No-one could force him to move on.

Fletcher. It's wrong.

Michael. Word has it he's on the prowl again. Had that Detective turn up on my doorstep out of the blue this evening. I knew something was up.

Fletcher. Are they re-opening the case?

Michael. No, she was all unofficial, off-the-record. I don't know what put the spooks into her all of a sudden, but she seemed to think she should let me know he was still around, and check if I'd seen him about.

Fletcher. Sounds almost like you're trying to scare me.

Michael. He stuck around all this time like he was rubbing our faces in it. It's ended up putting my wife in hospital.

Fletcher. Franklyn?

Michael. All the stress of it built up over the years and –

Fletcher. – you think he stuck around deliberately to get at you and your family?

Michael. I wouldn't put it past him. The cops said he was arrogant: always had the answer for everything; a picture of calm. But if he goes anywhere near my Ashley, I don't know what I'll do.

Fletcher. Yes, you do.

Michael. What?

Fletcher. I can see it. You know what you'd do.

Michael. I won't pretend I haven't thought about it.

Fletcher. There's no justice. I mean, surely you deserve something – some compensation. You should look it up.

Michael. Believe me, I tried. I had all the promises, all the lawyers begging me to make a claim. But 'insufficient evidence' put an end to that. No justice. I even thought about going to your lot – selling the story.

Fletcher. Tricky business. You know we can't publish anything that identifies the victim; especially not when it's a child.

Michael. As if the whole town doesn't know already.

Fletcher. I know, but rules are rules. *(Pause)* I'll tell you what I *can* do, though.

Michael. Go on.

Fletcher. I have eyes and ears all over the place. I can have them keep me informed about what he's up to. Anything comes up not connected with you, nothing to stop me running with a new story, is there? Look, here's my card. Hear anything; you let me know.

Michael. I don't wanna go stirring up a hornet's nest.

Fletcher. Leave the stirring to me. You just look after your wife.

Michael finishes his drink, picks up the business card, and exits. Fletcher waits; and exits.

Scene 9

Office

Cross. If you've come to have another go/ I'm not…

Bishop. … actually/ I came round yesterday to apologise.

Cross. Really?

Bishop. But then I hear you went to see Michael Edwards.

Cross. So that's why you're here. Do I need to justify everything I do to you?

Bishop. What possessed you to be so stupid?

Cross. I just went to see how he was.

Bishop. Don't insult my intelligence.

Cross. Do you know his wife is in hospital, in a critical condition? A coma, in fact.

Bishop. No. And I didn't know that because it is none of my business. Or yours.

Cross. How did you get to be so cold?

Bishop. Oh, please spare me the righteous indignation. It's not about being cold – it's about having boundaries. You have a responsibility not to cross the line.

Cross. I don't see compassion as crossing the line. And as for righteous: coming from you? Always here, breathing down my neck, protecting me from the big bad world.

Bishop. Or yourself.

Cross. I made a judgement call, ok? I acted on my gut instinct. Isn't that what you taught me to do?

Bishop. *(Softer).* Ellen – sit down.

Cross. I don't want to bloody/ sit down…

Bishop. …sit…/ down. *(Beat.)* We both know why you went to see Edwards, and it wasn't just compassion for a man whose wife is in hospital. Speaking to Franklyn and then going to see Edwards on the same day. Why are you doing this to yourself?

Cross. He just gets under my skin. I don't know why, but he just winds me up so much. I've had cases fall through before – we all do. But this one –

Bishop. – you have to let it go.

Cross. I can't. Something about Franklyn eats away at me.

Bishop. You respect him.

Cross. No, I/ don't…

Bishop. …you/ respect him because he challenges you.

Cross. Are you sure it's not just you that respects him?

Bishop. He's formidable. I respect his intelligence.

Cross. He's arrogant.

Bishop. Perhaps. But that's not an offence, is it? You can't convict a man for being arrogant, although God knows I would love to. Ellen, he gets under your skin because you want – you *need* – to beat him. And you didn't.

Cross. It's not a competition.

Bishop. Yes, it is! It's a battle of intellect, morals, philosophy, and you damn well know it. I love you and respect you, Ellen. Your tenacity, your devotion, your rock solid moral compass. Above all, I care about you for your weaknesses. A strong woman, and a fantastic winner – but you are a bloody awful loser. You lost that case, and you have got to accept it before it eats you up and spits your soul out on the floor for Franklyn to trample all over.

Cross. 'Insufficient evidence'. It's a giant, dirty finger pointing right at me. I must have missed something crucial, something simple.

Bishop. You missed nothing that wasn't there to be seen.

Cross. I thought I'd found everything there was to be found: witness statements; a character statement from his boss; Steven's account; even his younger brother told me –

Bishop. – all he knew. That's all you could act on.

Cross. Put yourself in Michael Edwards' shoes. You can still hear the pain in his voice now, the anger bubbling under the surface. Can you blame him? There was no justice, especially not with Franklyn sticking around. Now he has a wife in hospital. I can't even begin to think what the man is going through.

Bishop. And that is why you must be so careful. Do you really want to have his arrest hanging over your head if he goes off on a vigilante mission, seeking his own revenge?

Cross. No, but –

Bishop. – but nothing. Feeding your own revenge doesn't help either.

Cross. My revenge?

Bishop. The case cost you a lot more than a little dent in your Detective pride, and you know it did. But you can't project that onto a personal vendetta against Franklyn. Let it go.

Cross. I can't.

Bishop. You have to.

Cross. No, I can't. – There's something else.

Bishop. Oh, no Ellen, please.

Cross. I spoke to Ashley.

Bishop. Ashley?

Cross. The brother.

Bishop. When?

Cross. Yesterday. In the park.

Bishop. Ellen!

Cross. I saw Franklyn talking to him.

Bishop. Please tell me you weren't following him.

Cross. Look, that doesn't matter. I saw them, and I heard them.

Bishop. You are playing with fire and you *will* get burnt.

Cross. Franklyn gave Ashley his phone number.

Bishop. What? How do you know that?

Cross. He wrote it down and told Ashley to 'call any time'. I can't ignore that. The detective who failed to get a conviction of a paedophile watched the same paedophile give his phone number to the younger brother of his previous victim, and did nothing. How would that look?

Bishop. How it looks is not the issue.

Cross. It's everything. You keep talking of my
responsibilities: how does this one stack up?

Bishop. Did you tell Edwards?

Cross. No. He'd be hunting Franklyn down by now if I
had. But I can't ignore it.

Bishop. Pass it on.

Cross. I can't do that.

Bishop. You're treading on thin ice as it is with all this
'off-duty' overtime. And it's not as though you can
claim you were making a legitimate investigation
when you saw it. So, pass your concerns on.

Cross. But if I try to explain *why* it's important, I'll be
laughed out the station with my P45.

Bishop. Exactly. So, don't make this your problem.

Cross. What if he doesn't know?

Bishop. Doesn't know what?

Cross. That Ashley is Steven's brother. Franklyn never
met him four years ago. What if he doesn't know who
Ashley is?

Bishop. It's a small town – maybe he does, maybe he
doesn't. What difference does it/ make…?

Cross. … if/ he knows who Ashley is, why would he
risk talking to him?

Bishop. He could be playing a very dangerous game: we
both know he's capable. Don't try and get inside his
head again, Ellen. So, get uniform to keep an eye on
him. Hell, phone Crimestoppers, or the NSPCC
anonymously if you have to. Either way, you've got to
do something quickly before this all gets out of hand.

Cross. No. I have to find out what's going on. If
nothing else, I owe it to that family.

Exit.

David enters as the lights change.

David. It's one of the hardest things to build, and yet at the same time the easiest to tear down. Trust. You've got to know what it is they need in order to build the trust. You need to provide them with the attention, the time, an ear, your understanding. All too often they just want the answers to life's difficult questions. If you can help them to find the answers themselves, be their sounding board, be their confidant, then they will trust you. When they trust you, nothing is beyond your reach.

Enter Cross and Fletcher

Cross. The third stage of grooming is where the paedophile starts to fulfil a need in the child's life.

Fletcher. For what?

Cross. Attention, comfort, someone to talk to, a shoulder to cry on, even someone who can give the child anything their parents or carers don't – gifts, opportunities, experiences. Whatever he works out he can use to buy the child's –

Fletcher. – co-operation? –

Cross. – trust. As the relationship builds, he'll abuse that trust and use it to sustain their compliance.

Scene 10

Park

Ashley. Have you ever had to keep a secret?

David. Of course.

Ashley. Yeh, but even one you don't want to keep, but know you have to?

David. It's not a nice position to be in, is it?

Ashley. What do you do about it?

David. Well, I guess you have to ask whether keeping it will help or hurt anyone.

Ashley. What if telling will hurt someone too?

David. Why do you assume that telling the truth will hurt people?

Ashley. Because it will.

David. How do you know that?

Ashley. I just – do. You know, like, a girl asking you if she looks good, and you don't think she does. Sometimes you say 'yeh, you look great' because you know that telling her the truth right then is gonna hurt her feelings.

David. If you really thought she looked awful, would you let her go out like that, to save hurting her feelings? Or would you rather risk a little upset from your own honesty to save her a more public embarrassment later on?

Pause

Ashley. Is *not* telling the whole truth – keeping some things secret – is that as bad as lying?

David. It's called 'lying by omission': not the same as
    making something up, but more about holding
    something back.

Ashley. It *is* just as bad then.

David. The end result can be the same.

Ashley. So, what do you do when every choice seems
    like the wrong choice?

David. You simply stop. Put the entire of your world on
    pause and decide only about what is right and wrong
    in that single moment. The past has gone, and the
    future is yet to be decided. Don't try to pretend you
    have the power to right all the wrongs in the world –
    just do what it is you know you can do. Make the
    choice – take the action *you* can take.

Ashley. How?

David. *(Thinking carefully)* Imagine you are driving a car
    carefully down a narrow, one-way street.

Ashley. I don't know how to drive.

David. *(As if sat in a car)* Come on. Right, consider this
    your first driving lesson.

Ashley. *(Unconvinced)* Okay.

David. Steering wheel. Gear stick. Left foot: clutch – to
    change gears. Right foot: gas pedal and brake pedal.

Ashley. Right, okay.

David. So, you're driving down a narrow, one-way
    street.

Ashley begins to enjoy the mime, typically steering unnecessarily.

If you carry on swerving around like that you'll have the
    cops pulling you over, checking to see if you're drunk.
    Anyway, you're driving down a narrow, one-way

street, and a young child suddenly runs out in front of
your car.

Ashley. Shit!

David. What do you do?

Ashley. Hit the brakes as hard as I can.

David. What if you're not sure you can stop in time?

Ashley. Swerve to the side!

David. It's a single lane road, the paths are filled with
children walking home from school.

Ashley. Well, I don't know then. Hit the brakes and
hope. I don't know.

David. What if you have seen the car behind you driving
so close it is certain to run into the back of you if you
slam your brakes on?

Ashley. That's his problem. *(Turning around.)* – Back off,
you bastard!

David. In the car behind there's a young child in his
passenger seat, not strapped in – pretty much certain
to be killed if the car hits you.

Ashley. I don't know.

David. Decide. There's no guarantee you'll stop before
you hit the child in the road –

Ashley. I don't know –

David. But stop suddenly and the child in the car behind
will fly through the windscreen –

Ashley. I don't know – stop it –

David. So, decide – decide now –

Ashley. I can't! Fucking stop it –

David. Which one are you going to kill, Ashley? Which?

Ashley. Fuck off! Stop it!

David. You can't save them all – hit the one in front, hit
the ones on the side of the road, or have the one
behind hit you –

Ashley. Stop it!

David. What do you do?

Ashley. I don't know! I don't know!

David. Decide - decide now! Someone has to get hurt
either way – it's your choice – you are going to have
to face it either way – decide –

Ashley. *(Screaming)* STOP! I stop before I hit the kid in
front. It's not my fault all those kids are on the side of
the road, and it's not my fault that twat behind me is
too close and hasn't strapped his kid in. I have to stop
– that's all I can do.

Pause

David. Exactly. When life drops you into those
moments all you can do is slam the brakes on; do the
one thing that is within your control; the one thing *you*
can do to make it better; and leave the rest of the
world to make decisions or mistakes for itself.

Ashley. That's what I have to do, isn't it?

David. All I am saying is that when you don't know
which way to turn because each route seems fraught
with danger, all you can do is face what is right in
front of you and do right by that. But you are still
young Ashley so, please, cut yourself some slack.

Ashley. I have to go.

David. Okay.

Ashley. Thanks for the driving lesson.

David. No problem. And remember – if you need to
talk, call any time.

*Ashley exits. David makes notes in his notebook as Michael
enters. After a few moments:*

Michael. You just can't stop yourself, can you?

David sees Michael and gets up to leave.

Don't walk away from me.
David. I have nothing to say to you.
Michael. Got a lot to say to my kids though, haven't
you?
David. That was four years ago.
Michael. You tore my family apart. And now you're
trying to do it again.
David. I haven't been anywhere near your family: you
approached me.
Michael. I have stood here watching you brainwash
Ashley – so don't try and deny it.

David only takes a moment to realise who Ashley is.

I won't let you tear my family apart again.
David. The only thing holding your family together is
the amount of time you spend apart.

Michael moves towards David.

Go on – take your best shot. Lose control to show us all
how much control you're in.
Michael. Get myself on assault charges for scum like
you?
David. What grates at you the most? The fact that you
couldn't get me sent down, or that *both* your sons – it

now appears – had to turn to me to get the attention you couldn't, or wouldn't give them?

Michael. Attention? Is that what you call it?

David. No parent can watch their kids every second of every day, but you'd think they should have a rough idea what is going on their lives.

Michael. Why don't you just leave?

David. You are the third person in as many days to ask me that.

Michael. Then get the fucking message. You aren't wanted here, by anyone.

David. And yet both your sons turned to me.

Michael. I'm warning you. You're being watched.

David. Maybe I am not the one people should be looking at. A man with an abused son, a wife in hospital, and another son talking to paedophiles rather than going to school.

Michael. Careful, Franklyn. That detective told me you were back out on the prowl. She might not have done her job right last time, but she won't make the same mistake twice. You stay the hell away from my family. Understand?

David. And if they come to me? You know Ashley will, just like Steven did.

Michael punches David in the face.

Blackout.

ACT 2

Scene 1

Fletcher enters alone and begins reciting from a draft of his own article. David should enter at some point during the article.

Fletcher. 'A local father was forced to defend himself and his family yesterday by lashing out against *suspected* child molester, David Franklyn. The man admitted that he hit Franklyn in a heated conversation between the two men. Franklyn was charged with sexual assault of a local teenager, believed to be the man's son, four years ago. The investigation ended without a conviction when the Crown Prosecution Service decided to take no further action and dropped the charges. However, recent confirmed reports have revealed that Franklyn has been arranging private conversations with more teenagers during school hours.' *(To David)* How does that sound?

David. I think you'll be hearing from my solicitor.

Fletcher. All I needed was the word "suspected" and then it became factual, which makes it easier to publish in the public interest.

David. You wouldn't know what was in the public interest if slapped you in the face.

Fletcher. I certainly know what the public is interested in, though. And as for a smack in the face – how is your jaw, by the way? Tell me, will you be looking to

take any action against Mr Edwards? It would make
for a great twist in the story. *"Suspected child molester tries
to sue victim's father"*. Brilliant!

David. You're not going to publish anything.

Fletcher. I always thought it was a shame that Edwards
never got the justice he deserved.

David. Or the compensation he was really after by
morally prostituting his own son for financial gain.

Fletcher. You sound like you treat sexual abuse as a
kind of game; merely a subject for your clever
rhetoric.

David. As do you.

Fletcher. But what about the victims?

David. There's no denying the boy was a victim, but
what of, we don't yet know.

Fletcher. Oh, I think we all know, really. Conviction or
not. And when people find out what you have been
getting up to lately –

David. – there's nothing to find out, especially not from
you.

Fletcher. What makes you so sure?

David. Because you don't want Ellen to get hurt.

Fletcher. What the hell does that mean?

David. Drop the façade, Daniel. Man-to-man, I know
you care about her in a more than professional
capacity.

Fletcher. And what business is that of yours?

David. It might be in the public interest.

Fletcher. Don't be stupid.

David. You want to protect her, so you know she can't
afford to work herself up into another hopeless

attempt to convict me for a crime I never even committed.

Fletcher. Are you afraid of what she might find if she digs a little deeper?

David. No, but she should be.

Fletcher. She can cope with whatever new abhorrent facts she discovers about you.

David. My case is dead and should be buried. It should have been consigned to the cemetery of bad investigations from the outset.

Fletcher. Who are you trying to convince?

David. If you don't want to find skeletons, don't go digging up a graveyard.

Fletcher. What?

David. One day Ellen is going to dig so deep she's not going to like what she finds. Are you ready for that?

Fletcher. If that's some kind of veiled threat, you had better drop it right now.

David. I'm not the one wearing a veil, Daniel. You can look *me* straight in the eyes. But there is a hell of a lot that still hasn't been seen.

Fletcher. We'll find it.

David. If you want to help Ellen chase her demons, then you do that. Meanwhile, I'll keep an eye out and an ear open for the truth.

Exit

Scene 2

Edwards Home

Michael is on stage. Ashley enters from upstairs and immediately makes his way to leave, as if in a hurry.

Michael. Hold on a minute.

Ashley. Dad, I've got to go, I'll be late.

Michael. Just wait, I need a word with you.

Ashley. No, Dad, I've got to go. Can't we talk later?

Michael. If I tell you to wait then you wait. Sit down. – Where are you off to in such a hurry?

Ashley. School.

Michael. Really?

Ashley. What?

Michael. I know you've been skipping school. Where have you been going?

Ashley. Who told you?

Michael. *How I* found out makes no difference to me.

Ashley. It does to me.

Michael. Why?

Ashley. Because it does.

Michael. The school phoned me. So, where have you been going?

Ashley. Just around.

Michael. Around where?

Ashley. Anywhere but school, or here.

Michael. What's brought this on?

Ashley. Oh, I don't know. Could it be that I am worried sick about my mum, but you won't let me see her? I can't concentrate, so why bother going to school?

Michael. You can't just ditch school when things get a bit tough. It's like running away – it's not the answer.

Ashley. It was for Steve.

Michael. Have you even thought how your mum would feel about this?

Ashley. What's that supposed to mean?

Michael. Nothing.

Ashley. I do care about mum, you know. I want to see her, but you won't let me.

Michael. We've talked about this. I told you I would take you when I'm ready.

Ashley. It's always about you, isn't it? Everything – always what *you* want.

Michael. That's not true.

Ashley. Maybe I should just go live with Steve.

Michael. Don't be so stupid.

Ashley. So, I am stupid now, as well? I'm not your precious Steve, just your stupid little Ashley – is that it?

Michael. That's enough!

Ashley. Just the stupid little brother who doesn't mean anything.

Michael. I said that's enough.

Ashley. Yeh, stupid Ashley: all he has to do is keep his mouth shut.

Michael. Shut it now before I shut it for you! Only a stupid boy would skip school to spend time talking to complete strangers.

Ashley. What?

Michael. I know where you've been going: sitting in the park –

Ashley. – that cop told you, didn't she? I knew she
would.

Michael. Cross?

Ashley. She's a liar, just like everyone/ else…

Michael. …she/ knew about/ this…?

Ashley. …she/ promised she wouldn't tell.

Michael. That's why she came round.

Ashley. No, it wasn't. A minute ago you were saying the
school phoned you.

Michael. Well, yes, they also –

Ashley. – you're lying.

Michael. How dare you! Never call your own father a
liar.

Ashley. Why not? You are one. You lie, you make me
lie, made Steve lie –

Michael. – stop it, you ungrateful little shit. All I've
done for you and you have/ the nerve…

Ashley. …that's/ all you do, scream and shout. You
never shut up and listen.

Michael. You are really pushing it now.

Ashley. Mum used to listen to me. She'd listen now, too.

Michael. She's in a coma, Ashley.

Ashley. Doctors believe that people in comas can hear
you talking to them, and they can sense you being
there.

Michael. Where did you hear that rubbish?

Ashley. Surely it is worth a try – it might help her.

Michael. You can't help her.

Ashley. I'm going to see her.

Michael. No, you're not.

Ashley. You can't stop me.

Michael. The hell I can't.

Ashley. *(Screaming)* I want to see my mum! I am going to see her and tell her everything.

Michael. You're going to keep your mouth shut, boy, or it will hurt your mother.

Pause. Ashley is stunned into silence.

She is a very sick woman, and if you start upsetting her she could get much, much worse. Do you want that on your conscience, Ashley? *(Pause)* You're not going to see your mother, are you? – Good. You'll see your mother when I am good and ready. Understand? So, you are going to go straight to school, and then come straight home. And you will not speak to that man again. Ever. He is a very dangerous man, Ashley. He is the one who drove Steven away from us. – Yes, it's him. He is a danger to this family, Ashley. He wants to hurt us again, split us apart, and every time you talk to him you help him. Do you want to help him break up the family: to hurt your mother? Our home is our home and what happens here is our business, and no-one else's. Understand? – I'm going to get ready to see your mother. If you do as you are told, maybe I'll think about taking you to see her. *(Pause)* Ashley, I love you. And you love me too.

Michael hugs Ashley, but Ashley is clearly very uncomfortable. Michael exits. Ashley sits down. He takes the piece of paper David gave him out of his pocket and reads the number on it. He picks up his dad's lighter and motions to burn the piece of paper, but stops, closes the lighter and puts it in his pocket. Ashley stands, takes his mobile out and begins to dial the number.

Ashley. *(Very quietly)* Hello? I really need to talk.

Ashley Exits.

The lights change. Cross and Fletcher enter.

Cross. The fourth stage of grooming is all about lowering the child's inhibitions about sex.

Fletcher. How?

Cross. The paedophile will want to take small steps so as not to scare the child away or damage the trust. They'll bring the topic up in casual conversation, steering the child towards talking about it to see what their reaction is. Sometimes they'll initiate games or activities that involve undressing in an apparently innocent way. They may even begin to show the child pornographic material. Physical contact with the child will increase, slowly getting more intimate and personal.

Fletcher. Wouldn't the child feel uncomfortable or embarrassed?

Cross. Why? If they already trust their new, special friend who gives them so much, what reason would they have to question it? The more secrets they share, the more special the relationship feels. What child would want to lose that? Remember, the manipulative paedophile will spend time making the child feel safe in their presence so as to abuse that safety later.

David enters.

David. When they trust you, when they *really* trust you, they will turn to you for guidance on anything. Even the most personal and private of matters. Each time they reach out to you the relationship strengthens. It can feel like a whole new territory. The trust may be tested at times, boundaries can become blurred and confused, and you must keep them safe. Every child must be allowed to feel free to move from not knowing and not thinking, to becoming able to understand more about how they feel. How they feel about you. About themselves.

Scene 3

Park

Ashley enters and sits next to David on the bench.

Ashley. What happened to your face? You been in a fight?

David. No, it's nothing. *(Long pause.)* You're quiet –

Ashley. – I know who you are. My dad told me. He says you're dangerous.

David. Does he? Well, a lot of things have been said about me, Ashley.

Ashley. What's it like? Being called – well, you know.

David. To be honest, I'd rather be called a murderer.

Ashley. Oh.

David. Ashley, I also know who you are. And your dad. And Steven.

Ashley. Oh, right. But how long have you – ?

David. – I only *realised* yesterday.

Ashley. And you're still talking to me?

David. We're just two people sitting in the park talking.

Ashley. Can I ask you something personal?

David. Of course.

Ashley. Have you ever *done* anything?

David. Done what?

Ashley. You know, like everyone says.

David. And what is it that everyone says?

Ashley. I don't know.

David. Yes, you do. *(Tapping his head)* You've got the words right there. Sticks and stones may break my bones, but words can never hurt me. Isn't that what they say?

Ashley. It's not true, though.

David. No, it isn't.

Ashley. So, have you? I won't tell anyone.

David. You shouldn't keep secrets like that – especially not for adults.

Ashley. Why?

David. Whenever an adult gets a kid to keep a secret like that, it's because they know what they have done is wrong. You don't need to keep secrets for me.

Ashley. I already have.

Ashley gets out the paper with the phone number.

David. I never/ asked you…

Ashley. …I didn't/ save it on my phone because my dad checks it.

David. Sensible. That's for you – he doesn't need to know about it.

Ashley. You still haven't answered my question.

David. About what I did? What I've done? What do you think?

Ashley. I don't know.

David. It's actually refreshing to hear someone say that. Most people think they know.

Ashley. There's *one* thing I do know. You never did anything to hurt Steve.

David. You should keep that opinion to yourself.

Ashley. All I had to say to that detective was that Steve had changed since he met you. And the last time I saw him get back from the youth club he was upset. He'd been crying. Mum and Dad had a huge argument that evening. And then Dad phoned that manager of the youth centre – your boss, wasn't he? – they were friends. Then the police turned up and it all kicked off.

David. All that – it must have been hard for you.

Ashley. Steve did change, though.

David. I know he did.

Ashley. He told me what you did. He told me how/ you...

David. ...Ashley/ don't...

Ashley. ...he/ told me the truth. How you listened to him. Tried to help him. How he could only trust *you*. He hated *me*.

David. Why would he hate you?

Ashley. Because I lied.

David. Lied to Steve?

Ashley. Lied *for* him.

David. I don't understand. *(Pause)* You know you can trust me?

Ashley. Yeh.

David. Then *tell* me: what lie did *you* tell for Steve?

Ashley. You see, this is what I mean about hurting someone no matter what I do. If I'd told the truth years ago maybe I could have stopped it.

David. Stopped what?

Ashley. I can't.

David. What?

Ashley. If I tell the truth *now* people will get hurt.

Beat.

David. You remind me a lot of Steve.

Ashley. Don't say that.

David. Sorry. I didn't mean to –

Ashley. – I'm not like Steve. I wish I was.

David. Why?

Ashley. Because he's strong, and free from all this.

David. You're stronger than you think.

Ashley. But I'm not free, am I?

David. From what?

Pause. Ashley is looking David straight in the eyes, close to saying something, then backs down.

Ashley. I can't! I promised I would never tell.

David. It's ok. I won't make you tell me.

Ashley. So, what do I do?

David. I can't tell you what to do, either.

Ashley. If I could try to make things better, but without telling the – would that still make me a bad person?

David. You are *not* a bad person.

Ashley. But could it help?

David. Do right by what is in front of you. No more –
Ashley. – no less. You're right.

Ashley gets up to leave.

David. Where are you going?
Ashley. I've got to do something. I've got to try, at least.
David. Try what?
Ashley. I've got to try and slam the brakes on.

Exit

Scene 4

Office

Cross is in her office, rummaging around as Fletcher enters.

Fletcher. Is it safe to come in?
Cross. If you're here to fish for more information to
  bloody publish, I'm not in the mood.
Fletcher. Actually, it was just a social call.
Cross. I'm not feeling very sociable.
Fletcher. That's no problem: I can be sociable enough
  for the both of us.
Cross. Look, Fletcher –
Fletcher. 'There once was a copper called Cross' –
Cross. – I'm actually rather busy –
Fletcher. – 'Who spoke like she thought she was boss' –
Cross. – I'm trying to –
Fletcher. – 'I declared love' –
Cross. – get out –
Fletcher. – 'But she gave me the shove' –

Cross. – I'm not listening –

Fletcher. – 'Pretending she don't give a toss.'

Cross. Amusing.

Fletcher. Pun intended.

Cross. I'm sure it was.

Fletcher. Oh, Ellen, loosen up a little. You're more highly strung than an astronaut with a cello.

Cross. How kind of you.

Fletcher. Can't you just stop, even for five minutes?

Cross. Ok, fine. Five minutes. But I'm timing you.

Fletcher. You're not the first woman to say that to me. Anyway, come on, let's get you out of the office, away from work and just chill out for a while. It's Friday!

Cross. I see what is going on here. Did Ruth put you up to this?

Fletcher. What?

Cross. She did, didn't she?

Fletcher. No. That being said: I might find the old codger quite annoying, but she cares about you. We both do.

Cross. You're like broken records.

Fletcher. Ellen, this whole Franklyn thing could get really messy. I think he could be dangerous.

Cross. I'm not afraid of him.

Fletcher. He's so vengeful; you don't know what he is capable of. He's threatened me – threatened you.

Cross. When?

Fletcher. Earlier. I happened to bump into him. You do know Edwards saw him, don't you? Gave him a smack round the jaw, too.

Cross. What the hell?

Fletcher. Exactly! You've got Edwards starting his own
vigilante mission, and Franklyn talking about suffering
and pain and skeletons staring at you –

Cross. – skeletons? –

Fletcher. – just something he said. I don't like it, Ellen.

Cross. Hold on. Edwards saw Franklyn? Then he must
know who Ashley is. And Franklyn gave no indication
that he would stop seeing Ashley, or move away?

Fletcher. If anything, he sounded more determined.

Cross. Dan, I need your help with something?

Fletcher. This doesn't sound good.

Cross. I have to find out what is going on.

Fletcher. Walk away from it, Ellen.

Cross. If I find out what Franklyn is *really* up to, and I
can prove it, I'll pass it on. Okay?

Fletcher. How do I fit into this?

Cross. I want you to talk to Michael Edwards.

Fletcher. Why?

Cross. I need you to find out more about his wife.
Something in my gut tells me she is a major piece in
this puzzle.

Fletcher. I'm not sure I can do that in an entirely ethical
way.

Cross. Just do it, and don't tell me how.

Fletcher. But why the wife?

Cross. I want to know why Steven Edwards got so
drawn in by Franklyn four years ago.

Fletcher. Didn't you interview her back then?

Cross. We didn't need to. She sat in with Ashley when
we asked him some general questions, and we didn't
get much from the forensic interview of Steven.

Fletcher. So, how would it help to talk to her now?

Cross. It's just a hunch. The sooner I can talk to her, the better. Find out what her condition is and get me an idea of how soon I speak to her.

Fletcher. And all off-the-record?

Cross. Please Dan, help me do this.

Fletcher. Right, okay. But only because it is you. And what do I get out of all this?

Cross. I'll consider walking to Tesco with you.

Fletcher. What about the sausage roll?

Cross. Don't push it.

The office phone rings and Cross answers it.

Cross. *(On the phone)* Who? – On his own? – No, it's fine, bring him up.

Fletcher. Who's that?

Cross. Ashley Edwards.

Fletcher. What's he doing here?

Cross. I guess I'm about to find out.

Fletcher. Do you want me to stay?

Cross. No, you should go.

Fletcher. Ellen, that's not a good/ idea…

Cross. …he/ might not talk to me if someone else is here. It could be important.

Fletcher. But you know better than –

Cross. – I am aware of the risks, Dan.

Fletcher. Okay, okay. Look, take this.

Fletcher takes his small Dictaphone out of his pocket.

For your own sake.

Ashley enters.

Ashley. Detective.

Cross. Ashley, what are you doing here?

Ashley. I need to talk to you.

Cross. Sure. What's going on?

Fletcher. Ellen, are you sure you'll be –

Cross. – yes, Dan, let me deal with this.

Fletcher. Be careful, Ellen.

Cross. I'm fine. *(To Ashley)* Sit down. *(To Fletcher)* Just go
and do what we agreed? I can handle it.

*Fletcher exits. Cross presses 'Record' on the dictaphone before
turning back round to Ashley.*

Does your father know you're here?

Ashley. No way! But I bet you'll tell him, just like you
told him I skipped school.

Cross. I didn't tell him.

Ashley. Don't lie to me. I am so sick of all the lies.

Cross. I'm not lying to you.

Ashley. You have to listen to me!

Cross. I will listen, but you need to calm down. Maybe I
should call your dad –

Ashley. – no!

Cross. He should know you're here, really.

Ashley. Put the phone down, please.

Cross. But, Ashley –

Ashley. – *(Aggressive.)* you keep your mouth shut!

Pause. Ashley retreats, sits, sobbing.

Cross. Ashley! What's happened? Has – someone *hurt*
you?

Ashley. No. No, not me.

Cross. I don't understand.

Ashley. I lied. Everyone lied.

Cross. What did you lie about?

Ashley. You made me say those things about him.

Cross. Who?

Ashley. David.

Cross. Ashley, you shouldn't be –

Ashley. – he listens to me –

Cross. – but you shouldn't be talking to him. He's a very clever man: gets inside your head.

Ashley. No, he doesn't get *inside* my head, he helps me to get *outside*.

Cross. He's a dangerous man.

Ashley. Why does everyone want me to hate the wrong people?

Cross. What?

Ashley. He never did anything to Steve. I lied for you. I lied for –

Cross. Has he told you to say this?

Ashley. I don't understand why you wanted me to lie.

Cross. I never asked you to lie.

Ashley. But you never asked to hear the truth, did you?

Cross. What truth?

Ashley. David never did anything to Steve except listen to him and try to help him.

Cross. You're saying you lied four years ago?

Ashley. We had to. I didn't want to; I tried not to. I tried to just tell the truth, but you made it into a lie.

Cross. *(Unconvinced)* Ashley, that's a long time to hold onto a lie.

Ashley. Well, no-one was ever bothered about the truth.

Cross. I don't know what you want me to do.

Ashley. Leave David alone. He's the only one who seems to care at all about me.

Cross. No, Ashley, he only cares about himself. You might be a bright boy, but you have a lot to learn about people.

Ashley. You have to listen to me, believe me –

Cross. – I can't ignore what I know.

Ashley. Then listen to what you don't know!

Cross. I don't know how to, Ashley.

Ashley. You mean you don't *want* to?

Cross. Of course I want to. If I could, I would. But it's not that simple.

Ashley. Simple?

Cross. Yes.

Ashley. When the fuck is life ever simple? I can only put right what is just in front of me. All I need is someone to help me.

Cross. Maybe I'm just not that person.

Ashley. You won't help *me* because you would have to believe in –

Cross. – I do believe in –

Cr./Ash. You/Him.

Pause.

Ashley. You have to believe in *him*.

Cross takes Ashley's hands and kneels in front of him.

Cross. I'm sorry. I can't. To say I believe now would be to say –

Ashley. – that you were wrong? That you *are* wrong about him?

Cross gets up and turns away from Ashley. Pause. Ashley takes out the phone number.

If he doesn't care about me, why would he give me this?

Ashley puts the paper on Cross' desk and goes to leave.

Cross. Where are you going?

Ashley. Somewhere I should have gone in the first place.

Ashley exits.

Scene 5

Pub

Fletcher. Fancy seeing you here.

Michael. Ah, my friend. Good to see you again.

Fletcher. And you. How are things?

Michael. Why is it that bastards always get away with everything?

Fletcher. I guess that's what makes them –

Both. Bastards!

Michael. Damn right. I like you. You know what the world is all about? Bastards screwing you over and screwing everything up. – Tell me, do you believe that people should get what's coming to them?

Fletcher. I guess so.

Michael. I am talking cold-blooded revenge for what they did. You believe that?

Fletcher. It depends.

Michael. What about kiddie fiddlers? Paedos? Perverts? You think they should get what's coming to them?

Fletcher. Well, it's my job to make sure the public knows what they have a right to know.

Michael. Yeh? Tell the world what some sick bastard did to a kid? You'd do that?

Fletcher. As long as I had the facts, I can write a –

Michael. – you're a good man. They should know what these sickos are doing, and you know why?

Fletcher. Well –

Michael. – because no-one else is going to do anything. The Police do fuck all, except moan about evidence and all that. You just need the hard facts, right? Tell everyone what the pervert is up to and we all keep a look out and stop them. Isn't that right?

Fletcher. I guess so, but it's not always that simple.

Michael. When the fuck is life ever simple? I could tell you things that would make your skin crawl. You should do a report about perverts and what they can do to a family.

Fletcher. Maybe what people need to know is about your wife.

Michael. What?

Fletcher. Well, think about it, if people knew about her they'd stand up and support you.

Michael. It poisoned her. Destroyed her. None of this would have happened if we'd got justice.

Fletcher. She should give her side, when she gets better.

Michael. She didn't have a *side*; just knew what was what.

Fletcher. Did she give the police a statement in the investigation?

Michael. Said all she needed to say. *I made sure* the cops knew all they needed to know.

Fletcher. But think about it: if we did a story on her –

Michael. – no-one is talking to my wife. Ever.

Fletcher. Maybe it could help.

Michael. Not going to happen. And no police are getting near my family again.

Fletcher. It's just that, having her viewpoint could –

Michael. – she's gonna pay, you know?

Fletcher. Who?

Michael. That stupid, useless, bitch cop that screwed us over last time.

Fletcher. I'm not sure you can blame what happened on Detective Cross.

Michael. The hell I can't. Someone ought to put that bitch in her place. And that pervert.

Fletcher. Look, I've got to go. I really do wish your wife all the best. – Sorry, where did you say she's being treated?

Michael. St. Mary's. As they say, her fate is in the hands of the Gods now. – Anyway, are you gonna write that report, then?

Fletcher. I get the feeling it's going to write itself.

Exit.

Scene 6

Office

Cross enters with David, who is carrying a box filled with used notepads.

Cross. So? What are you doing here, Franklyn?

David. I thought I'd share something with you.

Cross. I really don't have time/ for this…

David. …you/ need to make the time.

Cross. I had Ashley here earlier. Was that your doing?

David. Don't be ridiculous.

Cross. I don't know what you've done to him but he is one very confused/ boy.…

David. …scared/ boy.

Cross. I'm not surprised, given your reputation. – *(Points to the box)* And what the hell is this?

David. This is my life for the past four years. Every day, every event, every witness: everything from the day I was first arrested by you.

Cross. You've been – for all this time? – You're obsessed.

David. A volatile mixture of obsession and paranoia. You see, you built an entire case solely on hearsay and speculation: *'similar fact evidence,'* as you call it. Trawling any scraps you could use to build the picture you've already decided you've seen. It's like taking pieces from several different jigsaws and forcing them together just because they have similar colours.

Cross. You make it sound like a personal vendetta.

David. You're still witch-hunting me – off duty – four years *after* the investigation.

Cross. And now you intend to persuade me with thousands of scribbled notes? Get help, Franklyn.

David. It's not *me* that needs the help. I needed justice. But what happened to *innocent until proven guilty*?

Cross. What about when the system fails and the guilty walks free?

David. *(Exploding)* The system *did* fail, and the guilty man did *walk* free! But not *me*. No, *I* am not free!

Cross. Just get out!

David. Look! Everything is here.

He pours all the notebooks on the floor.

Cross. Franklyn!

David. Every move, every detail, all here, here, and here. I'll lay it out for you: my whole fucking life.

He takes two more notepads out of his pockets.

This one: I wrote down everything about Steven when I was released on bail. This one: has everything I know about Ashley.

David puts the two notebooks on her desk.

Cross. I don't want to read your sordid secrets.

David. Did Ashley tell you *his*?

Cross. What?

David. Secret. No, I didn't think so. Steven never got the chance either. He was *so* close. And Ashley –

Cross. – is just a boy –

David. – who has been hurt by lies and is terrified by the truth.

Cross. Why are you doing this?

David. Because I know that *look*.

Cross. What look?

David. That look in a child's eyes. The look that says *'please'*. When they can't express what they think or how they feel, but they no longer want to hide it. And their shoulders sag under the terrifying weight of the world as they inhale their words. Quiet, uncertain, punctuated with anger, flickering with desperation. Their gaze drops down, slips to the side as if the answer is written somewhere just out of reach. Until suddenly their eyes fix on you and their soul threatens to spill down their face, slipping through their fingers as they lose grip on their thoughts. Through burning-red rage, or the stone-cold silence, you know, you feel, that gaze screaming *'help!'* The window to the soul; the gateway to the heart. Those eyes, that look – saying *'help me.'*

Cross. No. Don't you understand? It's what you think – it's what you want to see.

David. Why? Why would anyone want to see that pain in a child? How could they see it and do nothing?

Cross turns her back on David. She takes out the dictaphone and presses buttons to rewind.

You've seen it too, haven't you? You know what it looks like.

She presses play on the dictaphone and her conversation with Ashley can be heard as the lights change to a flashback. Ashley enters, taking over the dialogue at:

Ashley. When the fuck is life ever simple? I can only put right what is just in front of me. All I need is someone to help me.

Cross. Maybe I'm just not that person.

Ashley. You won't help *me* because you would have to believe in –

Cross. – I do believe in –

Cr./Ash. You/Him.

Pause.

Ashley. You have to believe in *him.*

Cross takes Ashley's hands and kneels in front of him.

Cross. I'm sorry. I can't. To say I believe now would be to say –

Ashley exits, leaving Cross in the same place. David moves in and takes Ashley's place, holding her hands as she lifts her head and meets his eyes.

I was wrong.

David. That look: can you see it now?

He gets up and goes to exit.

The mistakes we make do not define us: it is what we do about them that makes us who we are.

David exits, leaving Cross on the floor. She rifles through the notebooks and then stops. She turns back to her desk, picking up the 'Steven' and 'Ashley' notebooks. She flicks through them, stopping to compare pages.
Bishop enters.

Bishop. Ellen, I just saw – my God! What happened?

Cross. Franklyn.

Bishop. Why?

Cross. To show me all this. His whole life for the past four years. All of it written in these.

Bishop. Everything? Is he obsessed?

Cross. I don't know any more!

Bishop. That's it. I am going to put an end to this once and for all.

Cross. No, Ruth, please listen.

Bishop. I warned you this would happen again.

Cross. What? Come on, out with it! This is all my fault?

Bishop. It's not about blame.

Cross. The hell it isn't. Everyone wants something or somebody to blame for everything, and they all want it delivered to their armchairs, or spoon-fed to them in a seedy tabloid, or exaggerated exposé. So, I have to deliver –

Bishop. – at all cost? –

Cross. – sometimes –

Bishop. – spoken like a true martyr.

Cross. What?

Bishop. What is it you feel you have to give everyone else that you can't give to yourself?

Cross. Justice!

Bishop. And do they have it yet?

Cross. No.

Bishop. You now what? I can't watch you do this to yourself any more.

Bishop exits, leaving Cross in the office.
The scene cuts to Fletcher on the phone.

Fletcher. Hello, is that St. Mary's hospital? – Excellent.
– I'm phoning on behalf of my brother, Mr Michael
Edwards. His wife is currently at your hospital. – Mrs
Rose Edwards – Yes, Edwards. – I'm her brother in
law. Her husband asked me to phone and get an
update because he's – Well, he could have phoned,
but I'm just doing him a favour, he's – Yes, I'm sure
she is. – Of course I've spoken to him. – Sorry? She's
where? – Oh. Right. Okay. – No, no, that's – all I
need. – Yes, I will let him know. Thank you.

He hangs up. Takes a moment to think. Exits.

Scene 7

Outside

Bishop. Franklyn.

David. I'm sorry, do we know each other?

Bishop. I work with Detective Cross.

David. In which case, I really have nothing to say to you.

Bishop. And I will thank you kindly if you don't talk to
Ellen again.

David. I don't invite her attention – quite the opposite.

Bishop. What was your little visit all about, then?

David. That is between me and detective Cross.

Bishop. Oh, no Mr Franklyn, you don't get off that easy
with me. You might think you can throw your
intellectual weight at Ellen, but I met too many men

like you in my career to be even the slightest bit
impressed or intimidated.

David. Men like me?

Bishop. I'm not here to start debating social philosophy.

David. Then why are you here?

Bishop. I am here for Ellen's sake.

David. To fight her corner?

Bishop. There's no fight to have.

David. To throw in the towel then?

Bishop. You are a victim of your own arrogance.

David. At least you've acknowledged I'm a victim.

Bishop. Let it go, Franklyn.

David. Let it go? Do you have any idea how much I've
had to let go? How many opportunities passed me by
– *still* pass me by when people recognise my face?

Bishop. And does talking to lone kids in public parks
help that?

David. Don't be absurd.

Bishop. You're persistent.

David. So is she.

Bishop. You crossed the line.

David. What line?

Bishop. You know what I am talking about.

David. It bothers you, doesn't it? Someone being able to
defend themselves? Who can't be bullied.

Bishop. You're a paedophile.

David. Alleged.

Bishop. There's no smoke without fire.

David. Would you arrest a man who walks out of a pub
and drives away in a car?

Bishop. Not everyone drinks alcohol.

David. Would you arrest another man who puts his keys
on the bar next to his pint?

Bishop. You know full well —

David. — that having keys does not necessarily mean he
will *drive* away from the pub. So, you don't and can't
arrest either of them because no crime has been
committed.

Bishop. What's your point?

David. Yet with nothing more than hearsay, idol gossip
and speculation you'll brand the next man a
paedophile, guilty until proven innocent. His details
will mysteriously find their way to the press; his name
will be published; his reputation ruined; family
humiliated; and his life will be ripped to pieces. And
all that before he has even been charged for a crime
that might not have even occurred in the first place.

Bishop. You're cynicism doesn't make you right, or
prove your innocence.

David. Neither does your ignorance make me wrong, or
prove my guilt.

Bishop. We cannot start from a position of assuming
that everyone could be a liar.

David. Unless they've been accused? Then the *more*
intelligent, calm and collected a man is in his defence,
the *less* you believe them, regardless of truth or facts.

Bishop. Concerns for the safety of a child cannot go
unchecked.

David. Of course not! But when the blinkers are on and
all you see is the finish line you're bolting towards, all
your energy focused on winning, you don't stop to
question the hurdles in your path, you just leap right

over them without a moment's thought. Presuming guilt from the beginning leaves a stain on innocence by the end.

Bishop. There are always risks when working with children. You know that.

David. That's a pretty sick justification for all the lives ruined by false allegations.

Bishop. Compared to the justifications paedophiles give for sexually abusing children; I'd say it is more of a realistic assertion. But, okay, I'll humour you. Let's assume you are innocent.

David. How gracious of you.

Bishop. Surely you can understand that you must have done something that led to people's concerns, aroused suspicions, fuelled the fire.

David. And there it is again. Even in innocence, the accused are blamed for others' perceptions or lies.

Bishop. Society just wants children to be safe.

David. Then they should look closer to home. Our children are neglected and physically, emotionally and sexually abused far more often in the one place that goes unchecked until it's all too late. And yet, more people can name a famous celebrity accused of molesting children than can tell you how many abused children suffer or die every day in their own home. But which one is the better story? Which sells more papers, or gets more news coverage? When we can't even be trusted with the truth, should it be any shock what happens with the lies? For each one told there are so many genuine victims left to suffer as those who should be protecting them are too busy chasing the smoke. So, detective, don't try to tell me I am to blame for other people's lies, or what they cost.

Bishop. I'll give you this: you are an enigma.

David. If everyone really knew how easily they can lose everything they love and live for, we could end up with no-one wanting to teach, or support or care for our children.

Bishop. And what about you?

David. I never stopped caring, I just had to stop showing it. But right now, that doesn't matter.

Bishop. What are you going to do?

David. Finish what Cross failed to do four years ago.

As Bishop exits, David moves to the bench in the park. The lights change as Cross and Fletcher enter, stood either side of the stage:

Cross. The fifth stage. The paedophile takes the next step and the relationship becomes sexual.

Fletcher. Why wouldn't the child just tell someone?

Cross. Fear, guilt and confusion are all tools the paedophile uses to maintain control. The child might even feel they owe the paedophile their silence in return for all the things they have been given. They might even be convinced that the new experiences are good, in some way.

Fletcher. No?

Cross. And even if they know it is wrong, or just feels wrong, they would have been conditioned into the fear that telling anyone would only result in a lot of trouble: angry parents, confused friends, disgusted neighbours – and all of it would be their fault. For a lot of children, they simply fear that they won't be believed.

Cross and Fletcher exit as the lights focus on David, sat on the park bench, alone.

David. It's the ultimate decision you can make. To cast aside the risks to yourself and reach out to take a child's hand, pull them back from the precipice, catch them as they fall, or stand between them and their most terrifying enemies. Amidst the public hatred, poisonous rumour and the damnation of lies, can you still bear the thought of letting innocence suffer a lonely death? Can you save a child by daring to believe the truth?

Scene 8

Park

Ashley enters.

David. I was wondering when you'd show up. I was a little worried after our chat earlier.

Pause.

Ashley – what's wrong?

Ashley. Why won't anyone listen?

David. You didn't get what you wanted from Detective Cross, then?

Ashley. How did you know/ I'd…

David. …I went/ to see her too.

Ashley. Does she believe you now?

David. I appreciate your support, but you have your own life to think about. You are still so young. Your job is to wish and wonder, leave the worrying to me.

Ashley. I've grown up worrying.

David. And I know you're worried about your/ mum…

Ashley. …worrying/ what would happen when everything was all found out.

David. If this is about what you told me/ earlier…

Ashley. …it started/ before Steve even met you. I always knew dad loved Steve more than me, the amount of time they spent together. Dad always said it was because Steve was older. They had this secret between them, and no-one else knew about it.

David. I know.

Ashley. You know?

David. Steve was close to telling me about a *secret*.

Ashley. Why don't you hate Steve – and me – for what we did to you?

David. For a time, I thought I did. But deep down I knew Steve was just trapped in a much bigger, darker lie: and I always knew it was something to do with that secret. Just like I now know you also got dragged into it too; somehow.

Ashley takes his Dad's lighter from his pocket and begins to play with it, opening and closing it repeatedly, but not lighting it. There is a long pause and neither of them speaks.

Ashley. The first time it happened – we still shared a room. I woke up. I thought Steve was having a nightmare: all the moving around. I tried to look but I couldn't make out what the shadows were doing. Then I thought I heard really quiet whispering. Not a nice whisper. *'Do you like it? Do you like it?'* It didn't make sense. *'You love me too. Say it.'* And it went silent. All I could hear in the dark was the sound of dad's lighter. And Steve crying. My big brother, always the tough one, was crying into his pillow like a little kid. I wanted to ask him if he was okay. I opened my mouth, but nothing came out. We never spoke about it.

David. Did Steve and your dad know/ that you…

Ashley. …one night/ they stopped suddenly. The lamp switched on and the room lit up. I froze. I held my breath like you do at the top of a rollercoaster, you know, when you wish you weren't there, but you can't get out. Dad just carried on, staring at me all the time. I couldn't move. *'Let's just keep this secret between a dad and his sons, right?'* I couldn't – say anything. *'If you tell your mum it will hurt her.'* So, I didn't tell mum, or anyone. Ever.

Pause

If the truth hurts, but lies hurt more, what choice do we have left?

Pause.

David. I have always found that, in the long term, the truth is the only thing that counts. Even if it hurts in the short term.

Ashley. But what if no-one wants to hear the truth?

David. Some find it hard to take.

Ashley. I never thought anyone would believe me,
anyway.

David. I know how that feels.

Ashley. You believe me, right?

David. Of course I do.

Ashley. Why?

David. Ashley, you have done the bravest thing I have
heard of in a very long time. I don't know how you
found the courage to tell me, but I'm glad you did.
And no matter what anyone has told you, your mum
will be proud of you: telling the truth will not hurt
her.

Ashley. Nothing can hurt her now.

Ashley begins to cry.

David. Ashley, listen to me. You are not to blame. Look
at me! None of this was your fault.

Ashley. You're the only one who listened to me and
Steve. Thanks for that.

David. There's no need to thank me for what you
deserve.

Ashley. You don't work with kids any more, do you?

David. No, not since –

Ashley. – well, I'm sorry for all those other kids who
never had you there to help them.

Ashley gets up to leave.

David. Where are you going?

Ashley. Home.

David. But, Ash, we really should go and talk to
someone/ about…

Ashley. … why/ bother? It's too late.

David. No, it's not. And I can't keep this to myself. You understand that, right?

Ashley. Tell whoever you like. Who's going to believe *you* anyway?

David. It's not *me* they need to believe. It never has been. But you no longer have to face this on your own.

Ashley. *(Giving David the lighter)* Here, you take this. *He* won't need it any more.

David. I don't/ understand…

Ashley. … I'm/ sorry, I've got to go.

Ashley exits.

David. Ashley? Ashley!

He looks at the lighter, lights it, then closes it in anger. He takes out his phone, thinks, and then dials.

Scene 9

Office

Cross. *(On the phone)* Yes, that's fine, I'd like to speak to him anyway. Could you get someone to bring him up? – Thanks.

Cross hangs up the phone. She starts looking through the notebooks David gave to her on Steven and Ashley, stopping on a page in the 'Steven' book, and then beginning to leaf through the 'Ashley' book. Michael enters.

Michael. Detective.

Cross. Mr Edwards, I wasn't expecting to see you today.
Is everything okay?

Michael. I want an update on what you're doing about
Franklyn.

Cross. Officially speaking, I was/ just…

Michael. … I want/ that bastard locking up.

Cross. It's not that simple, you should know that.

Michael. Don't tell me what I should know. He
destroyed my family!

Cross. I know it must be difficult right now –

Michael. – don't patronise me!

Cross. I'm sorry, I have nothing else to tell you.

Michael. Just do your bloody job!

Cross. With all due respect, if there is no evidence to
support a charge –

Michael. You have everything you need.

Cross. We had statements, but no other conclusive
evidence.

Michael. What about the doctor that checked Steve? He
said there/ was…

Cross. …it was/ inconclusive. No DNA transfer on
either Steven or Franklyn meant there was no way to
forensically link them. You know this.

Michael. But he told you what happened. Or are you
calling him a liar?

Cross. It wasn't enough for the CPS. Their problem was
that Franklyn never had the opportunity to commit
the abuse Steven and you described.

Michael. Opportunity?

Cross. No closed doors, no isolated rooms, no private
conversations or time alone when they couldn't at

least be seen. No-one had the opportunity to do
anything to Steven without someone seeing, except –
Michael. – who? You're not planning on sticking your
nose into my family again, are you?
Cross. If I could get to talk to your wife when –
Michael. – if you or anyone else goes near my wife –

Cross reaches for the phone, but Michael beats her to it.

No, *Detective.*
Cross. I think you'd better leave.
Michael. I guess if I want something done properly, I've
got to do it myself.
Cross. Stay away from Franklyn.
Michael. You don't get to tell me what to do.

*Michael Exits, leaving a stunned and shaken Cross in her office.
She returns to the two notebooks for Ashley and Steven,
reading and comparing a page in them carefully.*

Cross. Shit.

Fletcher enters.

Fletcher. Ellen! Ellen, are you okay?
Cross. Edwards was here.
Fletcher. I just saw him leave. What happened? *(Picking
up the phone)* Did *he* do this?
Cross. It's ok.
Fletcher. Did he hurt you?
Cross. It's nothing.
Fletcher. I'll kill him.
Cross. No, Dan, leave it.
Fletcher. Ellen, he's been lying all along.
Cross. I don't know what or who to believe.

Fletcher. Do you know about his wife, too?

Cross. Know what? Is she awake? Can I speak –

Fletcher. – she's dead.

Cross. But – when did/ she?…

Fletcher. …she/ died in the accident. There never was a coma, Ellen. Edwards made it all up.

Cross. He doesn't seem like a man who's just lost his wife.

Fletcher. I don't think he is anything he seems.

Cross. But that means Ashley – he can't have known.

Fletcher. Why wouldn't Edwards tell Ashley?

Cross. I don't know. Unless – Edwards had to keep Ashley quiet.

Fletcher. You mean? –

Cross. – with threats that his mother would be hurt by the truth, or that she wouldn't believe him anyway. It's the sixth stage: the abuser maintains control by using promises or threats in order to continue the abuse. It was Michael Edwards. All along.

Fletcher. Hurting – you mean – his own son?

Cross. We must find Franklyn before Edwards does.

Fletcher. Can't you call him?

Cross. No, I don't have his – wait, yes, I do. His number. He gave it to Ashley on a piece of paper, and Ashley left it here earlier.

Fletcher. Why?

Cross. I don't know – here it is. *(Reads the paper)* Shit! *That's* why Ashley left it here.

Fletcher. *(Taking the paper)* But – this is the Childline number.

Cross. When I saw Franklyn give – well, I just assumed
– he said '*call any time*' – I thought he meant – oh
God!

Fletcher. Where did Ashley go when he left here?

Cross. I don't know.

Fletcher. Think. Did he go home, go to find –

Cross. – he said: '*Somewhere I should have gone in the first
place.*' *(Beat.)* He was going –

Fletcher. – to the hospital.

Cross. So, he'll know about his mum by now.

Cross' mobile rings.

Fletcher. Someone has got to find that boy, and fast.

Cross. Hold on. *(On the mobile)* Cross. – I'm a bit busy –
Who called? – When? – What was the message? –
Okay, thanks. – No, I'll deal with it. *(Hangs up)*
Someone just called the station with a message for
me: they're on the way to the Edwards' address. The
caller was *Daniel Fletcher.*

Beat.

Both. Franklyn!

Fletcher. But why use my name?

Cross. Because he knows he can't use his own. I'm
going there now.

Fletcher. I'm coming with you.

Cross. *You* made the call. We can't arrive together.

Fletcher. Okay, I'll follow you.

Cross. Fine. But keep your distance, okay?

Exit.

Scene 10

Edwards House

The room is dark. Ashley enters and pours himself a vodka, drinks it, and then goes upstairs. Michael enters and pours himself a vodka. Ashley enters slowly.

Michael. I didn't know you were in. Where have you been all day? – What's wrong? You look like you've seen a ghost.

Ashley. When were you going to tell me?

Michael. Tell you what?

Ashley. Why the fuck didn't you/ tell me…

Michael. … watch your/ mouth/ boy …

Ashley. … my mum/ is dead? She's dead!

Michael. You went to –

Ashley. – the hospital? Yeh.

Michael. I didn't know how to tell –

Ashley. – the truth? –

Michael. – my son –

Ashley. – you lied –

Michael. – his mum was dead.

Ashley. You killed her!

Michael. It was an accident!

Ashley. You fucking killed her!

Michael. The drugs –

Ashley. – the lies killed her.

Beat.

Michael. Ashley, I/ love you …

Ashley. … don't/ you say it! Don't!

Michael. I lost Steve, I lost my wife –

Ashley. – before she ever knew what you did to us.

Michael. I did nothing to *you*.

Ashley. You fucked my brother and made me watch!

Michael. Shut your mouth you stupid/ little shit.

Ashley. …you can't/ shut me up any more.

Michael. No-one will believe you.

Ashley suddenly lashes out at Michael, hitting and kicking him desperately, violently.

Ashley. I hate you! I hate you!

A loud bang on the door offstage.

David. *(Offstage)* Ashley! It's David, let me in!

Ashley stops for a moment and Michael takes the opportunity to regain control over Ashley. A violent struggle ensues, with Ashley trying to get away.

Ashley. *(Screaming)* David!

Michael. Shut up!

David enters.

David. Ashley?! – Let him go, Edwards.

Michael. Get the hell out of my house!

Ashley breaks free and runs to David.

David. Are you/ alright? …

Michael. …get/ your hands off my son!

David. *(To Ashley)* Wait outside: the police are on their way.

Michael. You're going nowhere, boy!

Michael moves to grab Ashley, but David stops him.

David. It stops now! He's already told me everything.

Michael. *(To Ashley)* You're pathetic!

David. I'm warning you.

Michael. Do you really think your mother never knew our secret, Ashley?

Ashley. What? Stop it! –

David. – don't listen to him –

Michael. – and she did nothing about it!

Ashley launches at Michael but ends up on the floor. Michael moves to hit Ashley. David grabs Michael and pulls him back.

Cross. *(Offstage)* Police!

Cross enters and goes immediately to Ashley.

Ashley, are you ok?

Michael. Get him off me!

Ashley. *(To Cross)* It's not David's fault.

Cross. *(To Ashley)* I know.

Michael. *(To David)* I'll have you done for assault!

David. I've been accused of far worse.

Cross. David, let him go!

David. Are you here to chase smoke, or to see the fire?

Cross. Just let him go – so I can arrest him.

David throws Michael to the floor.

Michael. Arrest me? You stupid –

Ashley. – no, dad! The lies stop!

David. Ashley? –

Ashley. *(To David)* – my mum –

Cross. – *(To Michael)* I know about your wife –

Michael. – you know nothing –

David. – *(to Ashley)* what is it?

Ashley. She's dead.

Cross. *(To Michael)* I know you lied about the coma.

David. He did what?

Ashley. She's – in the accident, she – she –

David. *(To Michael)* – and you lied about that? You sick, twisted –

Michael. – keep him away from me!

David. Don't you see what your lies have done?

Cross. Franklyn, leave him.

David. You want to see the fire, detective?

David grabs the vodka bottle from the side.

Do you want to see where the fire was burning all along?

Cross. I know, Franklyn, I see it now –

David takes hold of Michael and pours the vodka over him.

Michael. – do something!

Cross. Franklyn!

David takes out the lighter and flicks it open. Cross backs away, taking hold of Ashley.

Ashley. *(To David)* What are you doing?

David. I'll give you fire –

Cross. – put the lighter down –

David. – *(To Michael)* you feel it now? –

Michael. – Jesus Christ! –

David. – the fear –

Ashley. – *(To Cross)* you have to stop him!

David. *(To Michael)* Do you like it? Do you fucking/ like it?...

Michael. ...please!/ Stop! –

Cross. – you don't have to do this –

David. – say it –

Cross. – David! –

Michael. – I lied –

Cross. – I believe you –

David. – *(To Michael)* say it! –

Ashley breaks free and rushes towards David.

Cross. – Ashley, no! –

David. – it was you! –

Ashley. – *(To David)* Look at me! –

Michael. – yes! –

Cross. – Ashley! –

Ashley. – Please! –

Michael. – it was me.

Ashley. It's time to slam the brakes on.

Ashley closes the lighter. David releases Michael, who slumps to the floor, sobbing. Calls of "Police" come from offstage as Cross begins to usher Michael out. He can be heard objecting and protesting 'ad lib' as he exits. Other actors or crew can be used as police officers.

David. *(To Ashley)* It's over.

Ashley. Dad, I'm sorry!

David. Ashley, you have nothing to be sorry for.

Cross. Franklyn, I –

David. – just go. Do what you need to do.

Ashley. What am I gonna do? What about Steve? He still doesn't know.

David. Detective Cross will bring him home, *(to Cross)* won't you?

Cross nods and smiles at Ashley as David leads him to the door.

Can I? –

Cross. – yes, go with him. And, David, thanks – for the tip-off.

David. It wasn't just *his* eyes I looked into. Remember?

Cross. You weren't really going to –

David. – what do you think?

Cross. Honestly? I don't know what to think about *you* anymore.

David. Well, that's a good place to start.

David hands her the lighter and exits with Ashley. Cross opens the lighter and attempts to light it once, twice, a third time. She then looks at it closer, sees it has no flint, and closes it with a smile.

Epilogue

Fletcher. Suspected paedophile David Franklyn is being questioned by police in connection with an alleged '*breaking and entering*'. It is believed that the incident is linked to the charges of sexual assault brought against Mr Franklyn four years ago. Detective Sergeant Ellen Cross, who assisted on the previous investigation into Mr. Franklyn, gave the following statement:

Cross. I can confirm that Mr Franklyn is helping police with their enquiries into a suspected breaking and entering incident in the local area. In order to protect the identity of witnesses, we are unable to disclose any further details, or the address of the incident at this time.

Fletcher. Officers received a call from a member of the public reporting a disturbance. It is understood that a child may have been in the house at the time of the incident. – *(To Cross)* Vague enough for you?

Cross. Do you really have to describe Franklyn/ as a…

Fletcher. …if we/ want people to read the story, then yes.

Cross. But we both know that's not who he is.

Fletcher. Perhaps it's not *who* he is, but it's *what* he will always be *known* as.

Cross and Fletcher exit as David enters.

David. This compulsion, this drive, this energy that both moves us and incapacitates us at the same time. It tells our eyes what to see, our ears what to hear, and our heart what to feel. But whilst our hearts may drive us, our minds must be there to steer us cautiously through and past perception, in search of and towards the truth. To protect the innocence of our children, we must protect innocence for us all.

The End

Performance Licences

Applications for performance licences for *No Smoke* are welcomed from professional and amateur companies, including schools, colleges, and other educational establishments. The terms of the licence will be negotiated for each individual application. Not-for-profit, charity and educational establishments are encouraged to contact the writer at the earliest opportunity in order to ensure that financial or budgetary limitations do not prevent them from making an application.

Please respect the author's copyright:
No performance of any kind, including readings or excerpts, may be given by professional or amateur groups unless a licence has been obtained. This includes not-for-profit, charity and educational groups. Publication of this play does not necessarily indicate its availability for performance. Purchase of a copy of this play, via printed or digital means, does not constitute permission or licence to perform. Please contact the author if you would like to discuss obtaining a licence.

No Smoke
Copyright © Colin Ward, 2018
All Rights Reserved

info@inasmanywords.com
colin@colinwardwriter.co.uk

Other works by Colin Ward

Novels
To Die For

Poetry
Ripples: a Collection of Poetry

Short Stories
Stench of Death & Mulch

www.ingramcontent.com/pod-product-compliance
Lightning Source LLC
Chambersburg PA
CBHW021330060726
47591CB00006B/1955